REFLECTIONS ON INSTITUTIONAL CATHOLIC-ISM

REFLECTIONS ON INSTITUTIONAL CATHOLIC-ISM

A CRITICAL PERSPECTIVE

And all must love the human form,
In heathen, Turk, or Jew;
Where Mercy, Love, and Pity dwell
There, God is dwelling, too.

—William Blake

HARRY GAEL MICHAELS

PROLOGUE

Over the past several years, one revelation after another has come to light about priests sexually abusing children, as well as the complicity of their bishops and, indeed, the hierarchy of the Catholic Church. For centuries, there has been an entrenched, fortified mentality among the papal hierarchy that has encouraged secrecy. One wonders whether the Church can—or ought to—survive with such rigid, closed attitudes toward its own sins, or whether it must yield to the evolution of humanity, conduct an honest assessment of its abuses of power, and "clean house" for future generations who wish to cultivate the measures of its essential spirit. It can be alleged that the Church's systemic or institutional problems began when it invested itself with temporal, political, and magisterial authority through the so-called Donation of Constantine in the fourth century AD—a document that was later demonstrated to be a forgery.

INTRODUCTION

During the time of Emperor Constantine I (272–337 AD), there was a dispute over the temporal authority of the Roman Church. Before he died, it was alleged that Constantine—Emperor of the Holy Roman Empire—granted the popes, as inheritors of St. Peter, dominion over lands in Judea, Greece, Asia, Thrace, Africa, and the entire Western Roman Empire, while retaining imperial authority in the East. This so-called Donation of Constantine was later determined to be a forgery; nevertheless, beginning in the eleventh century, the Church used it to support its claims to temporal power.

Lorenzo Valla (1407–1457), a priest and traveling professor whom Alfonso V of Aragon appointed as his secretary, was charged with investigating the document's authenticity. Alfonso, frequently at war in Europe over unsettled territorial disputes with the Papal States, had an interest in exposing the

Donation as fraudulent. Valla conducted historical and philological research and found that the document used words and turns of phrase that did not exist in Constantine's time.

Even so, it was not until February 11, 1929, that the Vatican was recognized as a sovereign state by Benito Mussolini on behalf of King Victor Emmanuel III. Valla's essay had circulated as far back as 1440 but had been forcefully rejected by the Church. Since 1929, the Roman Church—led by the Vatican—has been regarded as a sovereign state with absolute religious and moral authority over its faithful.

In October 2012, in Ireland, Savita Halappanavar—a 31-year-old married woman who was about four months pregnant—died of an infection associated with a miscarriage. She could likely have been saved had the doomed fetus been aborted. Instead, her doctors did nothing, explaining that "this is a Catholic country," and left her to suffer in agony for days. Savita's death is one of a long line of tragedies directly attributable to the doctrines and policies of the Roman Catholic Church.

As a former Jesuit-educated Catholic myself, I am aware of the many good, progressive Catholics who make up the body of the Church. However, the

Church is not a democracy, and those who wish to hold the institution accountable for its errors have no voice or vote in its governance. The Church is a rigid oligarchy—a dictatorship like the medieval monarchies alongside which it once existed—and it remains an institution run by a small circle of conservative, rigidly ideological old men who make all the decisions and choose their own successors. Whatever individual Catholics may do, the resources of the Church as an institution are too often dedicated to opposing evolutionary progress and enlightened change throughout the world.

When the devastating exposure of sexual abuse and exploitation of children by priests and bishops broke in the news, I felt compelled to write a letter to the Archbishop of San Francisco, as follows:

January 2009
Your Eminence:

I feel compelled to respond to the recent "apology" by Pope Benedict XVI for the latest heinous behavior of priests in Ireland, Germany, and elsewhere—not to mention in the United States.

I wonder whether the Pope is aware that such statements by the papacy are becoming subjects of ridicule and derision because of the obvious insincerity of the Catholic hierarchy in doing anything substantial about the problem of priestly sexual immaturity and social pathology against children.

I don't think the leadership of the Catholic Church yet grasps the magnitude of the Church's long history of social pathology and corruption. The hierarchy's defensive posture—protecting its inordinate power over the hearts and minds of the faithful in matters of "faith and morals," which to a Catholic mentality is practically everything—prevents honest reform.

Has it occurred to the hierarchy that the power and adulation bestowed on a priest can be tremendously seductive? It may grant an immature and developmentally deficient man a sense of authority he would not otherwise have, and it has allowed such priests to go on murdering the spirits and souls of innocent children. Parents are often helpless in the face of these atrocities because they, too, were taught as children that a priest's power and authority are ordained by God and that it would be blasphemous to challenge what a priest says or does.

I am writing this letter because I care about the many faithful Catholics who are victimized by their faith in the Catholic Church and their unquestioned but misguided trust in their priests. I was raised in the Oakland Catholic schools and educated through college by the Jesuits in San Francisco, and I feel deep disappointment and a sense of betrayal toward the institutional Catholic Church. Catholics are often dissuaded from reading their history and challenging the priestly hierarchy, but I urge you to read the work of James Carroll on what must be done to reset the Church on its true course, which was, I believe, the original intention of Jesus.

Thank you for your attention to my letter.

Sincerely,

Harry Gael Michaels
University of San Francisco, Class of '53

REFLECTIONS ON INSTITUTIONAL CATHOLIC-ISM

The Mission — Parts I & II

BY HARRY GAEL MICHAELS

PART

I

Power
Infallibility
Obedience
LOVE & COMPASSION
Fear & Control
RENEW THE CHURCH
Faith, Dignity & Freedom

THE CRITIQUE
PART I

The mystic was back from the desert. "Tell us," they said, "What is God like?"

But how could he ever tell them what he had experienced in his heart? Can God be put into words?

He finally gave them a formula—so inaccurate, so inadequate in the hope that some of them might be tempted to experience it for themselves.

They seized upon the formula. They made it a sacred text. They imposed it on others as a holy belief. They went to great lengths to spread it abroad. Some even gave their lives for it.

The mystic was sad. "It might have been better," he said, "if I had said nothing."

Whenever I read this anonymous saying, I always wonder why Jesus never wrote anything down. After all, he was obviously a brilliant man. Everything we have about His life and experience is what was written down by the Apostles —Mark, Mathew, Luke, and John (and others whom the early Church fathers did not legitimize) — many years after His death. One wonders what the writers' perceptions, motivations, and agendas were at that time, and how those perceptions, motivations, and agendas have come down to us over the years as "the word of God" or "the word of the Lord," as uttered in the Catholic Mass after each reading. Writings by Matthew and Mark, such as the following, seem out of character with the main portrayal of Jesus. The Gospels of Peter and Paul are considered less reliable sources by the Roman Catholic Church than the former (although Peter was designated to be the original head of the Church), and other Gospels, such as that of Thomas, are not acknowledged as having any validity at all.

These excerpts from the Bible, allegedly from the mouth of Jesus, are difficult to clearly understand because they often appear as figures of speech, metaphors, and parables. Perhaps in those days, concepts were easier to understand if words were spoken that way; however, the interpretations are ambiguous. One interpretation, which seems quite psychologically sophisticated is that Christ saw that people were too caught up in replicating the erroneous perceptions of their elders and only tended to perpetuate these rigid beliefs, however, for one to ascend to his or her true stature as a fully functioning and spiritual human being they must sever the chords that bind them to parental authority and "stand on their own two feet" as the saying goes, striving for "individuation" in Jungian terminology. The same goes for the second scripture quote. It is as though Christ were saying that belief in Him was a total mental, emotional, and spiritual affirmation of Himself and His teachings and required total faith—even to the point of losing one's own sense of self to the exclusive affirmation of Christ. The following are the two excerpts from the New Testament of which I spoke that, to me, are very difficult to understand and accept. "Do not suppose that I have come to bring peace on earth. I did not come to bring peace, but a sword. For I have come to turn a man against his father, a daughter against her mother, daughters-in-law against her mother-in-law- a man's enemies will be the members of his own household. Anyone who loves his father or mother more than me is not worthy of me; anyone who loves his son or daughter more than me is not worthy of me; and anyone who does not take his cross and follow me is not worthy of me. "Whoever finds his life will lose it, and whoever loses his life for my sake will find it."

Matthew 10—34, 35, 36, 37, 38, 39

This sounds more like the God of the Old Testament rather than the character of Christ as the "Prince of Peace."

Another excerpt from the Gospel of Mark, which is accepted as preaching the word of the Lord, is as follows.

"And he said unto them, Go ye into all the world and preach the gospel to every creature. He that believeth and is baptized shall be saved; but he that believeth not shall be damned. And these signs shall follow them that believe; In my name shall they cast out devils; they shall speak with new tongues; They shall take up serpents and if they shall drink any deadly thing, it shall not hurt them; they shall lay hands on the sick, and they shall recover."

Mark 16—15,16,17,18

I don't deny that there is wisdom in the Bible. Still, some of it sounds contradictory to good sense and believability. It lends itself to a very convoluted and distorted way of thinking, and that could quite possibly lead to destructive belief systems, as in the justification for slavery in times past or religious cults that handle poisonous snakes as testimony to their beliefs.

During the Reformation in the early Church, a significant split emerged over the criteria for salvation. One persuasion held that salvation was merited through good works and charitable activities, while another held that salvation came from faith and the grace of God. The following quotes from scripture seem to go to the heart of the controversy, and there appears to be a contradiction here. In Romans 2:6, we find: "For God will reward every person according to what he has done, and in Romans 2:7, "Some people keep on doing acts of good works, and seek glory, honor and immortal life; to them God will give eternal life. Then, in Romans 4:16, it says, "And the promise was based on faith, so that the promise should be guaranteed as God's gift to all of Abraham's descendants—not just to those who obey the law, but also to those who believe as Abraham did." As noted above, there appears to be some equivocation in the passages from Romans. Did God mean this or that, or is the answer to be found not so much in the words as in the heart? The Bible has been handed down by generation after generation and through translation after translation. Is it any wonder that there are numerous interpretations and confusions? Scholars have poured over it and attempted to glean the truth of God's intentions. Variations of interpretation could be thought of as an effect of human development and the evolution of different levels of awareness, as well as the personal agendas of the authors themselves. History tells us that a myopic view of religion, if not balanced with reason and good sense, can result in fanaticism that can seek to destroy all those not of the same persuasion. In my view, this is highly contrary to the essence of religious faith, which is to develop and learn to love and accept one another in the spirit of Godliness rather than to wall ourselves off in defense of self-righteous persuasions.

The issues of faith and good works were not the only events prompting the sincere efforts of Martin Luther, himself a Catholic priest, to initiate the Reformation. There was rank corruption in the hierarchy of the Catholic Church. Bishops, Cardinals, and Popes, themselves, were given to inordinate temporal power, sexual promiscuity, and luxurious, self-indulgent living. At the same time, the faithful were told under pain of eternal damnation to repent and buy indulgences so they could stay out of hell. As I see it, the Church is about control of mind and spirit and inordinate power.

On the issue of free will, with reference to God's intentions, another question comes to mind. How can one exercise free will if our only choice is obedience or eternal damnation, as many of us were taught in our early religious training? How can obedience be demanded in such a way with fear of reprisal if one does not obey? Why not consider a choice to respect and obey because one is trusted and loved? Even the most faulted of us would offer a second chance at reconciliation if remorse and atonement were expressed following offensive behavior. What good is love and obedience if it is provided under such a coercive mandate? The God of the Old Testament seems wrathful and intolerant, and vengeful in this sense, not at all like the God that appears in the personhood of Christ. How could the God of the Old Testament be the same God of the New Testament unless it was a different perception on the part of the people through an evolutionary consciousness? God, it is often said, is a God of love, as though God were the grand archetype of the perfect parent-child relationship in a state of sublime unity. It seems to me that humans needed a personification of God, on the one hand, and an acknowledgement of God as an incomprehensible author of the universe, on the other. The former offers comfort, reassurance, and a sense of security, while the latter offers only profound mystery. I see nothing wrong with a multi-dimensional perspective of God—i.e., a personification of a projected human God of compassion, as well as an acknowledgement of an incomprehensible God and Author of the universe.

Carl Jung, the famous Swiss psychiatrist and author of analytical psychology, in speaking of man's relationship with God, once stated; "It seems to me that as the human race grows and develops it becomes more aware of the value of espousing noble values of love, consideration and dignity" and, it might also be added that Jung, himself, avowed his belief in God while stating that if there were no God humans would have to create one.

An old man, whom I greatly admired and respected, once said to me that "God is love," but not a benevolent father who protectively looks out for us. He is rather the origin of the power of love. If we turn towards the God of love, our being can be profuse with grace and made whole. It seems to me that the expression of God-like love is sometimes seen in the behavior of highly developed human beings. This God-like quality of love and its expression in kindness, compassion, and contribution seems to have infinite dimensions and appears to be the most remarkable thing about the human condition. It seems to proceed from parental instinctual expressions of lower animals, but in humans makes a leap beyond parental in an instinctive way to providential in an altruistic way.

I was taught in the Catholic Church —and, I assume, in most Christian churches —that God is benevolent and loving as a Father. Yet how could a benevolent and loving father who has unlimited power over all the universe allow an innocent child to suffer more terror and pain and horrible anguish in situations in which the child is abducted, sodomized, tortured unspeakably, and finally slaughtered? I think there could not be such a God because no human father would allow such a thing to happen if he could prevent it. Since we are talking about an infant or small child, the question of free will as a keystone to salvation cannot apply: I think, therefore, that the God that is taught in Sunday school is a human projective personification. Also, how could an all-loving, omnipotent, and omniscient God create individuals whom He knows beforehand are destined to go to Hell?

I also think reincarnation as an explanation for all this is a grandiose simplification and is only an easy way of dismissing all these questions. To simply say that such an infant is working out the errors of its past life so as to achieve perfection does not make sense in the light of the free will issue. To say that the infant in question had free will to choose the conditions under which it would be born to work out its destiny, but did not have free will in life to do anything about it, is nonsensical. I can't believe in a God that makes no sense. I prefer to believe it is not God that makes no sense, but it is those religions that teach such things that make no sense. It seems to me that our social concept of God must be an evolutionary one and one that is a needed projection of our own human condition.

Someone once said that the Old Testament must be looked at in the light of the maturation and evolutionary levels of those primitive peoples who composed it, as well as in the light of their own agendas and struggles for living, as in a mythology of a people who express their perceptions in metaphor. I don't believe God is a thunderous old man with a white beard sitting on a throne in heaven. I think it is the authoritative manifestation of love that comes through the human being whenever she/he show kindness and compassion for another human being. On the other hand, we also see the most devilish evil committed by human beings. I wonder if primitive man felt compelled to personify beings as good and evil such that concepts of good and evil suggested beings from a heaven or a hell emerged. Could it be that when primitive man experienced loss and devastation, as must be in the human condition, he associated this with a concept of "hell" to bring some order and hope to his life, and developed an idea of an eternal afterlife that would preclude such loss and devastation? Could this be the emergence of religious thinking?

If we take a page from anthropological studies, we find that the primitive mind could only look around and see that its place in the world was one of vulnerability to forces far beyond its understanding and control, and therefore it would understandably become dependent on religious rituals and God appeasing dogmas of one kind or another. It was reasonable for a primitive man to think that the mighty gods of pasture could be appeased if acknowledged and obeyed and offered sacrifices, much as a child (even an abused child) might attempt to appease and pacify a wrathful father. Even if their lives were blissfully satisfying, as it is described in some tribes of the South Pacific, there was always the threat of terrible typhoons that could devastate their homes and their lives.

When polytheism gave way to monotheism and people began to see that we were all fundamentally a shared and common humanity, there were aggressive movements to bring all peoples under the authority of a single fatherhood, so to speak, as in the Crusades, the Inquisition, and the Arab expansion into Europe. Our ancestors thought of the monotheistic God as "Our Father" in a Jungian archetypal sense, but still a father with the attributes of demandingness, obedience, and servitude, along with the threat of His wrath and vengeance if there was not obedience and sacrifices of blood. The concept of the all-powerful God as father translated into extraordinary powers bestowed upon natural fathers and kingly fathers.

The kings of Europe and the sultans and pharaohs of the Middle East were believed to acquire their sovereign power directly from God through divine right. Some thought they were direct descendants of God, even as in recent Japanese history.

Historically, even in early America (17th century), under the influence of religious persuasion, children as subjects were held to have no rights other than those permitted by the biological or God invested father. (As an aside, I think the remarkable story of Moses was that even though invested with God-like powers by his people, he was humble enough to make clear he was only trying to do what he thought God wanted him to do. In no way did he ever assert or invest in himself an identity with God. So much power was invested in the concept of the father that such individuals in early America had the right to kill their children for disobedience, and this was permitted under the religious and civil laws of the time in New England.

In the Catholic Church, priests are addressed as Father and have invested in them powers of virtual spiritual life and death over their believers. "Whose sins you shall forgive, they will be forgiven—whose sins you shall retain, they shall be retained." This is the essence of the sacrament of confession and in this case, a priest has the power of God to forgive sins and allow the individual passage to go to God if he dies at that time or, as in the case of a mortal sin, if it is retained, the individual may be cast into hell for all eternity. These are beliefs from my own childhood and my mother's childhood that illustrate the power of the priesthood. In addition, the priest, father, had the power to perform transubstantiation, which is to turn ordinary bread into the actual body and blood of Christ. In other words, the priest saw himself as having the power to bring God to his altar and to make him assume the semblance of a wafer of bread to be ingested by the believer.

In my opinion, these are heady powers. It should also be stated here that the concept of priestly power extends to even those with exceptionally anti-social behavior if validly bestowed by a Bishop. This tells me there is an extraordinary capacity for the fatherhood of the Catholic priesthood to compartmentalize holiness and evil in the same person without any sense of the destructive pathology or the need for responsible reconsideration. Consider the extraordinary, abusive, and soul-murdering power of the Catholic clergy, supported by the bishops, of priestly pedophilia. In her book, *Perversion of Power-Sexual Abuse in the Catholic Church*, Mary Gail Frawley-O'Dea, Ph.D., a Clinical Psychologist who was raised as a Catholic, makes the point that over centuries of Papal authoritarianism, the Catholic Church as an institution has built its power on sado-masochistic control.

In his book, *Addiction and Grace*, by Gerald May, M.D., he puts forth the following paragraph, which, I think, expresses part of my quandary about what the Bible teaches concerning the love of God and the notion of free will. He says, "It seems to me that free will is given to us for a purpose: so that we may choose freely, without coercion or manipulation, to love God in return, and to love one another in a similarly perfect way. This is the deepest desire of our hearts. In other words, our creation is by love, in love, and for love. It is both our birthright and our authentic destiny to participate fully in this creative, loving, and freedom of will, and it is essential for our participation to occur."

Well, this all sounds very neat and tidy, but it does not explain situations in which, for example, the frantic and awful anguish of the parents of a small child, who had entered this world without arms, legs, vision, or hearing. The parents had brought this child to me as the staff psychologist, for the Diagnostic School for Neurologically Handicapped Children, and who implored me to discover some hidden ability or capacity for learning so that this child might participate in the grand scheme of freely choosing to learn and love and exercise a free will as to earning its salvation—which, of course, I couldn't do.

It seems to me that all the theologizing and philosophizing and religious dogma I have ever heard does not begin to explain such a life. The fact that some religious persuasions claim to answer such questions in pat dogmatic terms seems to me arrogant and untenable.

It is often said that the crucifixion is the highest expression of Christ's love for humanity; however, the crucifixion could also be viewed as a consequential result of Christ's life because the way in which he died was the culmination of a political confrontation with the magistrate of Roman rule at the time. It seems the Jews (the Sanhedrin) at that time were threatened by Christ's seeming assumption of appearing as the Messiah-which to the Jews was not what they expected and to assume that the Jews, as an entire nation crucified Christ and therefore were to be forever guilty of murdering Christ/ God and looked upon as deserving eternal damnation is a gross mis-judgement throughout all of history). So, according to history, the Jews brought him before the Roman magistrate (Pilate) for trial as an imposter and for appearing to claim personal sovereignty over Caesar's authority.

What was most important, in my view, was not how he died but what he taught within the realm of his own sovereignty. In those days, you could have expected anyone to be put to death by crucifixion (the standard way for executing criminals against the state) for announcing any personal sovereignty over the authority and "divine province" of Caesar, That Christ died on the cross to expiate our sins that were bestowed upon us by our original parents, Adam and Eve, seems to suggest that Christ's suffering was an atonement and reconciliation for man's transgression. It seems to me that Christ's purpose was not to come and show how much suffering he would endure for the sinfulness of man, but rather, in spreading a new sense of what it means to be human and what we all could learn from his example.

It further seems to me that the most essential words He uttered during his suffering and death were His expression of despair when He said, "Father, why hast thou abandoned me?" and then His other last words, "Father, forgive them for they know not what they do." To my way of thinking, these words express Christ's deep compassion and identity with the human condition. He knew feelings of despair and abandonment as a man and yet, He also ascended into Godly compassion when he acknowledged that man's sinfulness was mostly through ignorance and lack of understanding. This was the Godly compassion of Christ, who would teach forgiveness, so unlike the God of the Old Testament, who condemned the whole human race for an act of disobedience.

If one can believe that Christ rose from the dead and through His life and death made it possible for us all to "rise from the dead" and have eternal life as corporeal as well as spiritual beings, then it throws a whole different light on everything and reconfigures the end of man—or does it? How do we explain the end of those of the Old Testament who came before the Eucharistic Sacrifice and expiation of Adam's transgressions against the God of the Old Testament? How could the God of the Old Testament (who presumably is the God of the New Testament) condemn all of humanity that went before (except for Noah and his clan)? These condemned people, as I see it, who didn't even have the benefit of Christ's enlightened teachings, were only human like us, and probably no more faulted than we, even with the benefit of Christ's teachings. It seems that, on the one hand, God offers hope and love and, on the other, He is vengeful, demanding of unreasonable, and uncompromising obedience and quick to condemn-suggesting again that the difference between the old Biblical and the new Biblical concept of God is more the result of Man's psychic evolution to a greater sense of awareness of God as the emanation of compassion and understanding rather than the Supreme Administrator of harsh laws.

Even good human beings are not that way. Do we really believe that some people who lived then were so evil that God had to wipe them all off the face of the earth or might this have been an agenda cast by the early Jews who wanted to preserve only their own clan and claim all others were not of the "chosen people," whether or not something happened or didn't happen in the Bible (Old Testament) as it has come down through generation after generation and translation after translation seems rather not to be relevant.

Why do we place so much value on trying to understand what it says? Because it is the word of God, or because we have been told it is the Word and only the Word of God? In a sense, the matter of faith and choice in believing and respecting the intelligence God gave us is to want to live a good life and to espouse what our collective lights reveal to us as we move toward greater and greater understanding of God's magnificent universe. Whether one takes the book of Genesis as a literal, God-inspired story of creation or as an allegory of how our ancient ancestors viewed man's condition and place in the world, the Christian religions appear to interpret the story as an explanation for why there is suffering and evil in the world.

As the story goes, Adam and Eve were to love and praise their God, and in return, God would provide for Adam and Eve and their progeny a life completely unfettered by sickness, pain, death, or anything that would detract from an existence of total bliss and intimacy with God. Only there was a stipulation to this perpetual state of bliss and love. Man must obey God's command not to eat of the fruit of a particular tree, the "tree of the knowledge of good and evil," otherwise there was, literally, hell to pay. Man would be driven out of the Garden of Paradise and the blissful relationship with God and into the land "East of Eden," where there would be suffering, death, and every kind of wretchedness.

It seems that the only way Adam and Eve could show their love and devotion to God was to obey His command. Obey and live or disobey and die. But, and here is the rub. What kind of love could be of any value if it is required under such duress?

Even in our human lives, we can see that love is of very little value if it is not offered freely and without coercion. How could an all-loving, wise, and omnipotent God exact such a harsh punishment that belies any possibility for a naive and trusting man and woman to learn from their mistakes? And how could these original human beings be held responsible for the misery and suffering of their progeny, generation after generation, other than the usual interpersonal difficulties that most human beings must grapple with? How could such a God condemn His creation in such a brutal and abrupt way and then later decide to reconsider by sending Jesus to atone for man's transgressions and give him another chance at the Godly kingdom? God may not be bound by time, but we are, and we are creatures of God. So how, in the first place, could an all-knowing, omnipotent, omniscient, and loving God create people whom he knew beforehand to be destined to go to hell?

It seems to me that faith is all-pervasive, cultivated in one's faith compact with parents and the local community, and stemming from one's early experiences as a child. Faith is like an optimistic disposition and a conviction that ultimately all is well in the universe, that there is purpose and meaning and goodness and love in the authorship of our Creator or Divine Authority. It underlies all the basic attitudes perceived by the infant: that all is good because he/she is cared for in the most elemental needs (physiological, safety, basic trust, and reliable dependency and belonging), or that all is not good because of continual deprivation of those needs and helpless agitation.

Faith is inculcated through very early involvement with a significant caregiver with whom the infant forms a reliable, dependable attachment. This faith attachment is either reinforced by the caregiver's positive regard or negatively extinguished. The value of either grows by degrees as the child learns and experiences. The more the infant is cherished and cared for, the more faith it will have that all is well. The more it is neglected or abused, the less faith will be established and the more intense and twisted its chosen belief system may become. Belief systems, on the other hand, seem to be more of a reaction to fear and instability. Since an infant is by nature a social/human animal, it must absorb a reliable faith or its spirit might well become buried beneath a trash heap of chaos and self-doubt that eventually could lead to its destruction and/or the destruction of others. It appears to me that beliefs are built on a dearth of faith because it is the nature of the human animal to need something reliable, predictable, and dependable, something that confirms his existence and offers predictable ways to see the world. As I see it, faith is fundamental, and belief systems are acquired as compensations and predictable guide-posts to a perception of the world as a threatening place.

These needs seem to be so great that when commonsense tells us that a belief is contrary to rationality or destructive it, nevertheless, will be defended and preserved at almost any cost. It is the attitudinal conviction that says, "This is the way I want to see the world," regardless of what reality tells me. It is the choice to frame one's existence in what offers the hope and promise of what is valued, whether good or bad. Belief systems develop from a compulsive need to control, subjugate, and use coercive obedience. Belief systems come about from our experience with the world and its events in a negative sense, especially from fear. It seems to me that beliefs have to do with dogmas, doctrines, rigid rules, and a slavish and mindless obedience to what has been laid down in the past through an authoritarian power system (We just always did it that way, or it's what I was taught as a child). Faith, on the other hand, is based on trust and courage and freedom to grow, and a high regard for the dignity and value of human life.

On the face of it, one could gather that, according to the Bible, God gave us free will and then prohibited us from using it without coercion, i., the threat of terrible punishment as is taught by most Christian religions. How then can one invest one's most sacred faith in such words because they allegedly come from God? Must we believe the story as it is told, or is there a venerable truth in the substance of the words that are worthy of our trust? I think it can be seen that there is wisdom in these words if we consider that our early ancestors were telling us, in their primitive way, that man, indeed, has a relationship with God, however one conceives it. It seems to me that the ancient wisdom is telling us that human life has God inspired order and that if we follow that order, we will have a full and purposeful life; if not, we may fall into a life of hellish consequences.

We often see this developmental fugue played out during adolescence, when a young man or woman, in their quest for personal identity, willfully strikes out against their parents' best admonitions and well-meaning advice. Even the child in the stage of the "terrible twos" will show a belligerent defiance of parental authority at times to assert himself or herself toward personhood. We now understand that parents can in such instances of childhood defiance and disobedience (self-assertion) soften the child's struggle with understanding and respect by offering the child the opportunity to make choices between options and then hold the child responsible for the choice, acknowledging, of course, that the child must learn from its mistakes—rather than be made to feel inferior, inadequate or unworthy for them. The child then learns to trust and respect the parent, and love and faith can flow without the tragedy of tyranny and rebellion. Hence, adolescents can either make a smooth transition to adulthood and its concomitant responsibilities with trust and confidence in life's tasks, or they can unhappily lurch forward into a perceived hostile world of doubtful and untrustworthy authority figures.

I think the story of Adam and Eve can be seen as an acknowledgement on the part of our distant ancestors that we are, indeed, creatures of the Almighty and that it is in our best interests to accede, not to blind and intimidating obedience, but to a thoughtful and willing acquiescence to the love of God who promises a good life if willing to turn in grace and harmony toward the God of the universe as a flower will turn toward the sun as to be nurtured and bloom, or on the other hand, a wretched life if one turns away through stubborn willfulness and arrogance. In case of child abuse and destruction, I don't believe that it is "God's Plan" to subject a child to such evil ordeals. I don't think it is the reincarnated spirit seeking perfection and willing to submit to unspeakable torture as a simple explanation for an errant past. I believe these are unfortunate accidents of nature from which we can learn. They are tragedies and soul-wrenching events when they happen, but one can believe that such children are immediately taken into God's realm, where their new state expiates any suffering or anguish they may have felt on earth, as though it cannot even be remembered.

As I see it, the problem with Catholicism today is the schizoid disposition that Catholics must take if they are to defer to Papal authority. At the same time, use their God given intelligence to make their own decisions and thoughtful judgments about essential matters of living, procreation, and dying. When I was young, my understanding of being Catholic meant that you absolutely had to believe and accept without question all the dogmas, doctrines, and traditions of the Church. You also had to accept that the Pope, since the mid-1800s, had to be regarded as infallible in proclamations of faith and morals. Well, just about everything, to a Catholic, is associated with faith and morals. To consider oneself in disagreement with any of this meant you were not a Catholic. Furthermore, you were heretical and in danger of dying in a state of mortal sin, which meant eternal damnation in the fires of bell. In modern times, people are not burned at the stake or slaughtered or tortured in unspeakable ways, so you might say the Church has become more humanized.

Nevertheless, one associates with Catholics that still seem to fear Godly reprisal if they read about Church history or question the wisdom of the Church fathers. I do not see this coercive obedience as the way of Christ. I do not see that He was about rules, unquestioned obedience, and pompous (ostentatious display of dignity or importance) authority. In my opinion, the Church has not taken full responsibility for the evils of its past. If it did, it would change the internal structure of its authority and power. It would see itself as a society of compassion and forgiveness—especially of itself—rather than as a compulsive ruler. But it cannot forgive itself unless it first acknowledges its guilt, remorse, and wrongdoing.

However, it is gratifying to learn that in 1954, the Pope sent a Vatican delegate on a trip to Libya with these written instructions: "Do NOT think that you are going among Infidels. Muslims attain salvation, too. The ways of Providence are infinite." The Church, as it has come down through the centuries, has generally not represented the character of Christ. He was about love and the dignity of man to be truly good and sovereign as He was. He was not about worldly power, palaces, robes, and control of the minds and hearts of his faithful. As James Carroll has said in his book, *Toward a New Catholic Church,* what is required is "fundamental changes in the way history has been written, theology has been taught, and Scripture has been interpreted."

And, "if Argentina can repent, as it did in June 2000, of having offered refuge to Nazi war criminals, why can't the Vatican repent of having helped some of those same war criminals escape to Argentina?" says Carroll. Furthermore, he goes on to say that "the Sacred of Jews," the tradition of which the Church, despite its best intentions, is still custodian, simply must be more fully rejected. Peace depends on it." I find it difficult to trust a church that casts an insidious pall and influence on my spirit and that of my mother, who was taught to believe, as I was, that she was obeying the will of God by doggedly adhering to the rules and mandates of her church.

As I see it, the Catholic Church has posed as the exclusive guardian, preserver, and steward of Christ's spirit and, indeed, His body and blood. However, in my view, the visible and structured aspect of the Church has forsaken true Christianity for political and theological power and control over the minds and hearts of those who adhere doggedly to the bosom of the great "Mother Church."

I agree with those who say that the true spirit of Christianity is not to be found in theology and mind games of religious fixations, but is found in the simple and child-like trust and faith in the goodness of Jesus. I do not believe one can codify and bureaucratize spirit and expect the grace of God to come through the administration of meaningless rituals and traditions. It seems to me that Jesus taught that the obsession with rules and laws was squelching the God given dignity of the people, so they would go like sheep in mindless lockstep obedience in the name of a covenant with God.

I don't believe the core and spirit of life, as taught by Christ, was to be made up of stultifying traditions conjured up by some old men sitting under an olive tree or by self-righteous theologians trying to figure out how many angels could sit on the head of a pin. I believe Christ was teaching that we are creatures made in the image of compassion, dignity, intelligence, and society with our fellow man in creativity and a desire for oneness with universal authorship -not to a blind obedience to an authoritarian, bureaucratic hierarchy. The rules and doctrines of the Church are never open to question, and that, in my opinion, is an error.

The following are quotes from reviews of *Vows of Silence: The Abuse of Power in the Papacy of John Paul II,* by Jason Berry and Gerald Renner, about a former Pope up for a declaration of sainthood. "Vows of Silence is one of the most important books to appear on the current issue of priestly child abuse. It is a carefully documented work- consistent with the highest standards of journalism. The authors lay the blame squarely on the papacy of John Paul II, who appointed the Bishops and who mishandled the crises and who protected and openly promoted and protected those, like Fr. Maciel, the founder of the cult-like Legion of Christ, who are key to understanding its acute harmfulness and worldwide scope.

—Rev. Richard P. McBrien, Crowley-O'Brien, Professor of Theology, University of Notre Dame, and author of the book titled *CATHOLICISM.* "A chronicle of hard truths that show why the Catholic Church must undergo reform—or burial. Berry and Renner address their tragic subject with wide knowledge, impressive research, courage, and an authentic love of the Faith. Everyone who reveres the memory of Jesus Christ, or who cares for justice, should read this book."

AlterNet publishes original content as well as journalism from a wide variety of other sources and is a project of the non-profit Independent Media Institute. Its mission is to "inspire citizen action and advocacy on the environment, human rights and civil liberties, social justice, media, and health care issues. It was launched in 1998 and is funded by individual donations, grants from major donors, and advertising revenue. In 2001-2005, the top three financial backers of the Independent Media Institute were the Nathan Cummings Foundation, the David and Lucile Packard Foundation, and the Ford Foundation. (Wikipedia)

The following are many reasons, published by AlterNet, as to why the Catholic Church ought to do some self-examination and spiritual reflection on the character of its institution:

* Throughout the world, Catholic bishops have engaged in a systematic, organized effort to sign confidentiality agreements and quietly reassign the predators to new parishes where they could go on molesting. Tens of thousands of children have been raped and tortured due to this conspiracy of silence.

* Cardinal Joseph Ratzinger, who later became Pope, was personally implicated in a case from the 1970s in which three sets of parents reported that a priest in his diocese had sexually abused their children. In response, the priest was assigned to therapy, and without notifying law enforcement, Cardinal Ratzinger washed his hands of the matter. That priest was back on duty in just a few short days and went on to molest more children.

* When Pope Benedict XVI was Cardinal Ratzinger, he got a letter from the diocese of Oakland asking him to defrock a priest who had acknowledged molesting two children. Ratzinger ignored the letter and its several follow-ups for four years. Finally, in 1985, he wrote back saying

that more time was needed. Then they had to proceed very slowly to safeguard "the good of the Universal Church in light of the young age of the petitioner," by which was meant not the victimized children but the pedophile priest.

* Cardinal Ratzinger wrote a letter *De Deliclis Gravioribus* to all Catholic bishops, advising them how to handle accusations of sex crimes by priests. There were no recommendations to contact the police; instead, the instruction was for the bishops to report such cases only to the Vatican and tell no one else.

* Some Church officials, like the American Friar, Benedict Groeschel, have blamed the epidemic of child molestation on sexually wanton boys who tempt priests into assaulting them.

* The bishops threatened to cut off funding for immigrants' rights advocates. Preventing immigrants from getting legal and medical aid is less important than ensuring the Church isn't contaminated by even indirect contact with anyone who helps gay people.

* As sign of how ridiculously disproportionate and unhinged the Church's martyrdom complex is, Benedict compared expanding the rights of women and gay people to the murderous anticlerical violence of the 1930s Spanish Civil War.

* The bishops have used their official UN observer status to team up with Islamic theocracies like Iran and Libya to oppose calls for family planning Services to be made available in the world's poorest nations. They have gone to desperately poor and ravaged regions of Africa to spread the life-destroying lie that condoms don't prevent transmission of HIV.

* In the mid-twentieth century, the Vatican appointed a special papal Commission to study whether Catholicism should permit the use of birth control. When the commission almost unanimously recommended that it should, they ignored the recommendation and doubled down on their absolute ban on contraception. The Papacy excommunicated the doctors who performed an abortion on a pregnant 9-year-old who her stepfather had

raped. They did not excommunicate the stepfather.

* Savita Halappanavar wasn't the first: Catholic run hospitals are willing to let this woman die rather than get a lifesaving abortion, even when a miscarriage is already in progress and no possible procedure could save the fetus.

* In Poland, the Vatican ordered politicians to vote for a law banning In Vitro Fertilization and threatened to excommunicate anyone who didn't comply. The Vatican demanded that Catholic Sunday school teachers sign a loyalty oath agreeing to submit, "by will and intellect," to the proclamations of Church leaders.

* The Vatican has cracked down on American nuns for doing too much to help the poor and not enough to oppose gay marriage, and condemning them for displaying a seditious "feminine spirit". In Germany, where parishioners pay an officially assessed tax rate to the Church, they've tried to blackmail people who don't want to pay the Church tax and threaten to fire them from jobs in Church

institutions. In some cases, if the person opts out but later wants to re-establish their tax status and loses the paperwork, they demand on-the-spot repayment of decades of back taxes.

* In America, bishops have compared Democratic office holders, including President Obama, to Hitler and Stalin, and have said that it jeopardizes a person's eternal salvation if they don't vote as the bishops instruct them to do.

* The bishops fought against equal marriage rights for same-sex couples. It's not enough for the Catholic Church hierarchy that they refuse to perform Church weddings for gay and lesbian couples; they want to write that prohibition into the civil law and deny marriage equality to everyone who doesn't fit their religious criteria and have invested vast amounts of money and effort into doing so.

* In the 2012 election cycle alone, the Church spent almost $2 million in an unsuccessful fight to defeat marriage equality initiatives in four states. They have compared gay sex to pedophilia and

incest and called for it to be forbidden by law, saying that "states can and must regulate behaviors, including various sexual behaviors."

* They have shut down adoption clinics rather than consider gay people as prospective parents. The Church's official position, apparently, is that it is better for children to remain orphans or in a foster care facility than to be placed in a loving and committed same-sex household. They told a teenager he wouldn't be allowed to go through confirmation because he posted a pro-gay rights status message on Facebook. They expelled a preschooler from a private Catholic school because his parents were lesbian.

* They have a history of dumping known pedophile priests in isolated, poor, rural communities where they apparently assumed that local people wouldn't dare complain or that no one would listen if they did.

* When the Connecticut legislature proposed extending statute of limitations laws to allow older child-abuse cases to

be tried, the bishops ordered letters to be read during Mass, instructing parishioners to contact their representatives and lobby against it. To fight back against and intimidate abuse-survivors' groups like SNAP, the Church's lawyers had filed absurdly broad subpoenas demanding the disclosure of decades' worth of documents.

* When a Catholic official from Philadelphia, William Lynn, was charged with knowingly returning predator priests to duty, his defense was to blame those decisions on his superior, Cardinal Anthony Bevilacqua, thus acknowledging that the corruption reached to the highest levels of the Church.

* When confronted with hundreds of complaints about child-raping priests spanning decades, a Dutch cardinal used the same "we knew nothing" excuse once given by Nazi soldiers. Several months later, it was reported that this same Cardinal had personally arranged to move a pedophile priest to a different parish to shield him from accusations.

* After all this, the Church has the audacity to plead for money and ask parishioners to pick up the tab for legal costs and settlements.

* They tried to have an Indian skeptic, Sena Edamunuku, charged with blasphemy and imprisoned for debunking a claim of a miraculous weeping statue.

* The Vatican finances are a disorganized mess, lacking strong accounting controls and clear internal separations, which means parishioners who give to the Church can have no assurance of what the money will be used for. According to an investigation by "The Economist, funds meant for hospitals, cemeteries, and priests' pensions have been raided to pay legal fees and settlements in several diocesan bankruptcies.

* The Vatican has announced publicly that the sexist prohibition on women becoming priests is an infallible part of Catholic dogma and hence can never be changed. They have silenced priests who call for the ordination of women and other desperately needed reforms, exhorting them

to instead show "the radicalism of obedience," and they have excommunicated at
least one priest for advocating the ordination of women.

*   When it comes to the question of who is
financially responsible for compensating
the victims of sex abuse, they argue that
priests aren't employees. Therefore, the
Church bears no responsibility for anything they do.

*   They canonized Mother Teresa for doing
little more than offering a squalid place
for people to die. Outside observers
who visited her "Home for the Dying"
reported that medical care was substan-
dard and dangerous, limited to aspirin
and unsterilized needles rinsed in tap
water and administered by untrained vol-
unteers. The millions of dollars collected
by Mother Teresa and her order, enough
to build many advanced clinics and hospitals, remain unaccounted for.

In my opinion, the Church has not taken full
responsibility for the evils of its past and recent history. If it did, it would change the internal structure

of its authority and power. It would see itself as a society of compassion and forgiveness—especially of itself—rather than as an unreflective and obsessive ruler. But it cannot forgive itself unless it first finds genuine remorse and acknowledges its own guilt and wrongdoing.

The Church, as it has come down through the centuries, has generally not represented the character of Christ. He was about love and the dignity of man to be truly good and sovereign as He was. He was not about worldly power, palaces, robes, and control of the minds and hearts of his faithful. As James Carroll has said in his book, *Toward a New Catholic Church*, what is required is "fundamental changes in the way history has been written, theology has been taught, and Scripture has been interpreted."

I find it difficult to trust a Church that casts an insidious pall and influence on my spirit and that of my mother, who was taught to believe, as I was, that she was obeying the will of God by doggedly adhering to the rules and mandates of her Church. As I see it, the Catholic Church has posed as the exclusive guardian, preserver, and steward of Christ's spirit and, indeed, His actual body and blood.

However, in my view, the visible and structured aspect of the Church has forsaken true Christianity for political and theological power and control over the minds and hearts of those who adhere doggedly to the bosom of the great "Mother Church."

I was raised in the Roman Catholic tradition by a devout Irish mother and a dissenting Armenian Orthodox father, who chose to pursue the way of science and reason rather than that of a belief system. I say belief system because I draw a distinction between faith and beliefs, and that is the substance of this essay.

I prefer to use a non-Biblical definition because I think that faith and beliefs predate Biblical thinking. These concepts are indigenous to the human psyche, as is religion itself. Faith, on the one hand, or a belief system, on the other, are in my view, either the affirmation of life as a child finds it through parental caring or the lack of it leads to fear and despair as a sequelae or affective consequence and, therefore predisposes the child toward an attitude of socialization and community cooperation or an attitude of threat and defensiveness.

Faith enables a child to view life with a positive and forward-looking sense of value and reliability rather than a regressive attitude of nihilism and isolation. Faith is an attitude of trust. Faith is fostered through encouragement and love. Beliefs, on the other hand, are instigated, quite often, through fear and threat. The tender attitudinal engrams of early childhood are essentially established and once set are generally molded for life unless one struggles to individuate oneself toward personal sovereignty and self-determination as professed by such professionals as Carl Jung, M. D. and Victor Frankl, M. D., Ph. D.

In other words, what is authentic faith is that which emanates from one's spirit rather than the inherited and superimposed learned belief systems of the parents, which are often imposed through fear and guilt and sometimes even violence, as seen in the early history of the Roman Catholic Church, which is regarded as a pillar of Western Civilization.

I think beliefs, quite often, are established through fear and threat, as described by Abraham Maslow, Ph, in his book Motivation and Personality as the "psycho-pathogenesis of threat" in one's early developmental years, and this is why so much dissention and violence occurs in defense of beliefs. Beliefs are like living behind walls in a defensive manner, while faith is like living in the open without fear. So many of us live behind walls. It becomes a "them or us" kind of attitude that divides rather than unites people.

When what we call homo-sapiens or Man first appeared as a species distinct from primates, they must have struggled with their identity because finding themselves in an uncomfortable environment with threats all around them in the form of violent weather, threatening animals, and the struggle for sufficient food and protection from the elements, in general. In other words: "Who am I and what can I be doing here?" As these creatures were born, they must have been nurtured and cared for by their parents as a natural impulse for survival as a species, or neglected and treated brutally with abandon.

It seems likely that those who were accepted and nourished with warmth would be inclined to form social groups and cooperative communities to advance their best interests. In contrast, those who had been from hostile groups were motivated to wrest, from those more fortunate, what they felt they were entitled to, much like the gangs and mobs of today.

Our early ancestors would not have had any conception of a Deity. Still, they would have been aware of their vulnerability to threats around them. They would have recognized how little power they had against lightning, thunder, the elements, and powerful animals. It would seem reasonable that they would have attempted to beseech these powerful forces in some ritualistic way and, therefore, established communal methods of appeasing the great powers.

Even the parental influence of faith requires courage to maintain and develop because, as one encounters adversity in life, it takes courage to trust the faith that sustains. Beliefs can crumble with instability, while those seeking power and authority discover that imposing belief systems can become an instrument of control, much as the investment of the "Divine Right of Kings" and the absolute control exercised by the Papacy over its "faithful" for centuries, enabling a family or a Pontificate to govern with absolute power and authority over the masses.

From as far back as King Hammurabi (1792-1750 BC) of the Babylonian Empire, people were ruled by the threat to the established code of obedience. Punishment of some sort relative to a person's status was mandatory so that order and commerce could be maintained. Life was harsh, and very few people had the luxury and comfort to act civilly, and those who did often took advantage of and abused those less fortunate. Even during the emergence of Jesus of Nazareth, who taught that there was a better and more dignified way for people to live and value themselves, there was the oppressive Roman dynasty and military forces that made financial and power arrangements with members of some of the oppressed and more fortunate Jewish leaders to share in the indulgences of the time.

Jesus was perceived as a threat to the established order and was ultimately executed for that reason. He was a threat to the Roman establishment because he challenged the supreme authority of Augustus Caesar, the adopted son of Julius Caesar. He was also a threat to the established Jewish conciliatory power base, along with the Biblical belief that Jesus was claiming to be the Messiah, who biblically was believed to be a strong, military figure who bad the power to overthrow the oppressive Romans and liberate "God's chosen people" so they could inhabit and dominate the Holy Land. Their covenant with God promised this.

As I see it, the evolution of Man through the ages has been a constant struggle for survival, so resources of every kind have been focused in that direction. That meant building fortifications and military forces to protect against possible aggressors who would take what you had if they thought you had what they lacked for survival. It was only when a tribe thought it had enough essential resources and protection that it felt secure enough to reinforce its culture with things that enhanced its livelihood, such as inventions, significant architectural structures, and artwork, all of which further improved its lives.

Up to that time, it was rare for anyone to feel safe enough to think of much other than survival, so not much attention was given to the art and benefits of effective child rearing and implanting ideas of an affirmation of life and an appreciation of the wonderment and compensations of worldly existence, which I call faith. On the other hand, children were taught beliefs composed of thoughts about the successful ways our ancestors survived and about how our elders have propitiated the gods or God to sustain us through our trials and tribulations.

Sustaining tribal solidarity with firm belief systems to build absolute loyalty and fidelity to the tribe became recognized as an absolute necessity to maintain unity and cohesiveness. You were either in or out. If, by chance, you were fortunate enough to have had a secure upbringing and felt free to contemplate the wonders of the universe and condition your mind toward grander things, then you might encounter clashes with the established authority, as was the case with such historical figures as Copernicus, Galileo, and Michelangelo. A good example of what I am talking about is the clash between these previously mentioned individuals and the established Papal authority of the time.

History is replete with examples of such clashes between those who would adhere to the established authority and be ruled by the beliefs of the elders, and those who wanted to live in freedom and self-direction so they could appreciate the wonders and opportunities of life and what possibilities of advancement were possible. This may be at the bottom of what incited our revolution of 1776 and all past revolutions, as discussed in Fareed Zakaria's most recent book, *Age of Revolutions.*

I have often wondered why we have such divergent political/ social views on how we structure our lives—why we have liberal and conservative, sometimes in such extreme divergent vectors that compromise and resolution become almost impossible to resolve for at least some benefit for the general population, as is the purpose of our legislatures and political leadership. The exception, it seems, only comes in times of National threat, as it did in WWII, when all the U. S. coalesced and became a unified force to defeat the Axis powers whose intent was to conquer and impose their will and authority on our homeland and way of life.

Then why, in times of "peace," do we breed such internal conflicts and dissension that dire competition emerges rather than cooperative bipartisan civility? Look what has happened today when a venerable Republican political party has come under the influence of an unethical business tycoon by the name of Donald J. Trump, who is currently (April 20, 2024) being prosecuted in a New York Federal Court for the crime of an unlawful disposition of a $130,000 payment for prostitution services. He is also under indictment for three other major federal crimes in three different jurisdictions. This may seem off the subject, but this man, Trump, is again running for President of the United States as head of the Republican Party, and we, the people, must decide. Do we want to follow such a man and his disposition toward autocracy, or maintain and support our Democracy?

First and foremost, let me briefly define what is meant by autocracy on the one hand and democracy on the other. According to accepted definitions, autocracy is a government in which one person, or in some cases a few, such as an oligarchy, has virtually unlimited authority over others, akin to that of an absolute monarchy. This has been the case in most societies in the ancient past, and it was not until revolutions began occurring that political thinking began to change. Ancient Egypt was an example of an absolute and stable autocratic government.

Democracy, on the other hand, is a system of government in which all the eligible members of a Nation or Tribe are governed by their elected leaders who, in turn, are subject to dismissal if not proven worthy of those positions. A democratic form of government is usually intended to overthrow an oppressive, autocratic, or dictatorial (repressive) form of government, as occurred during the French and American revolutions.

I intend to throw out some controversial notions that I admit will likely spark disagreement. My intent is to generate thoughtful discussions because I do maintain that we come closer to the truth when we look at an issue through many lenses and facets. We are, after all, an organism of humanity that comes from one original reality, what we normally call God, the ultimate truth.

I think I understand what the Pope meant when he made the statement on Facebook some time ago. He said, "The Catholic Church is not an institution. It is a love story." This may or may not have been a response to my criticism of the Roman Catholic Church. I sent him a copy of my essay titled, *Reflections on Institutional Catholicism—A Critical Perspective.* My book was a response to the way in which the institutional/authoritarian structure of the Catholic Church has created disturbing conflicts for Catholics, especially in the areas of "faith and morals," because there is no flexibility or accommodation for the natural evolution of Man's consciousness and need for individuation of character development.

Catholics are seriously dissuaded from questioning, criticizing, or evaluating the tenets of the institution of the Church for fear of losing one's immortal soul and being condemned to an eternity of horrible suffering in bell with a loss of everything one has ever known to be good. Even though we live within a political structure that separates Church and State, the way of the Church is in existential contrast to our current form of government under the Constitution of the United States of America, which guarantees freedom to pursue happiness through liberty to think and speak as one chooses.

Our Constitution does recognize and guarantees that Church and State be separate in recognition of the different domains of authority and administration, and that is good, but it does show that the democratic form has flexibility built in to accommodate change and evolution, while the Church does not.

It may seem audacious of me to send my thoughts in writing to the papacy; however, I thought that since the Pope is a Jesuit and I was so educated, and besides, he seems like an approachable and thoughtful person. Furthermore, the Jesuit President of my own University agreed with me that the Catholic Church (that is, the people who comprise the Church) has long suffered from the need for a serious reform of the institution. It seems to me that what is missing are the spiritual treasures and moral/ethical values that constitute the true spirit of Christianity, as taught over two thousand years ago by a truly holy man from Nazareth who claimed a son-like affinity with his perception of a father-like God of compassion and understanding.

I take issue with the Catholic Church as an authoritarian institution because I was raised in that persuasion. I found such teaching as hell and satanic threats as odious and pointless because it seemed to me that our behavior was motivated more by fear, guilt, and the anxiety of staying out of eternal damnation than by a more constructive attitude of goodwill and positive regard for our neighbors, forbearance, and a wholesome attitude toward ourselves and life.

It seemed to me that the Vatican authority was established as a mechanism of power and control to maintain an uncontestable dominance over its believers. This was accomplished by implanting such ideas as strict obedience to the Church dogmas, through the administration of sanctimonious priests, in the minds of very small children, which, coupled with fears of hell, would bind them for life in that persuasion. This is what I mean by a belief system that facilitates a need for an autocratic director and leadership in life. In adulthood, one would either aspire toward a need to lead in this matrix of life or become a follower.

It does seem to me, however, that there are roots of love, compassion, and goodwill in the Church that emanated from its spiritual origins through the holy ministrations of Jesus of Nazareth before it became a religious/political institution during the time of Constantine I and his influence.

Under his leadership as the Emperor of the Holy Roman Empire, and the one who called for the Council of Nicaea in 325 AD to settle the question of Arianism, which was whether Jesus of Nazareth was truly identified as one with God or a mortal man. It was during this time that Constantine granted the newly established Papacy the power to engage in temporal and civil affairs as well as domain over vast territories of Judea, Greece, Asia, Thrace, Africa, and the entire Western Roman Empire, while leaving Constantine with imperial authority in the Eastern Roman Empire with the seat of his power in Constantinople. This, then, led to the great schism of 1054 over the issue of Papal power.

I do not place evil in the world as coming from a demon or satanic influence that exists in a person, such as the "Devil,"nor do I believe in a God who would create such a destiny for His creations. In my opinion, evil comes from within ourselves through ignorance and twisted pedagogical influences in our developmental years.

I want to quote from a source that I thought expressed an interesting view on the nature of God by the author, Vincent Bugliosi, as a child in parochial elementary school. His book is titled, *Divinity of Doubt,* in which he cites an event in his childhood. He said, "One day, the priest came in to visit our classroom and told us how good God was. I asked the priest, "Why, if God is all good, would He put people on this earth who He knew were going to end up in hell?" The priest's answer was that "God gave us all free will so that we could choose to go to heaven or hell and that God was not responsible for the choice that we make."

"Yes," I said, "but if God is all knowing, He still knows what path we are going to take before we take it, so I still don't understand why He would put people on earth that He knew were going to end up in hell?" The priest had no answer, was befuddled, and so he just walked out.

My Irish mother was raised as a Roman Catholic and very devoted to her Church protocols, although I think she was victimized by it as well. My father, a Ph. D. Biochemist, was raised as an Orthodox Armenian Catholic but did not practice a religion in any way as an adult. My early religious training was from the parochial elementary schools, mostly, and then the Jesuits through high school and college. I know what it is like growing up in an authoritarian religion (belief-based) vs. a scientific (reason-based) family environment, and since the authoritarian way was mandated by my mother's Church, I was raised in that persuasion.

I think what the Pope was referring to when he said, "The Church is a love story," is the bright side of the Papacy and all autocratic systems of life, in which those who accept what that system offers are relieved of having to struggle with their own existential questions and moral/ethical values. It is already laid out with a promise of eternal paradise if followed obediently—the Papacy in particular, because of the direct perceived link with God through Jesus of the Cross.

Autocratic systems are a way of providing patriarchal or fatherly protection and emotional security in an unstable and threatening world. Still, in a system that such a matrix offers, you must surrender one's own freedom to think and evaluate the realities of life, along with self-regulation, without fear of going to hell.

Not everyone wants to live that way, so we often have psycho/religious conflicts over it that frequently divide us into an "us and them" kind of thinking or "you're either with us or against us" as in ancient times, which has led to brutal wars and crimes against humanity.

I think the days of patriarchy and "fatherly" protection are coming to an end, much as it has been in the political realm, such that authoritarian autocracy is giving way to democratic self-rule; however, some of us struggle desperately to hang on to the old ways. Note the recent attack on our own Washington, D.C. Capitol building while our elected officials were exercising the most profound duty of their office by certifying the electoral votes for President of the United States, by a mob of warring "protesters" that were willing to destroy and even kill to retain what they believed were the safeguards of their emotionally secure way of life.

We must recognize that we are all creatures of a God of universal dimensions, not as we were taught as children of a personalized "fatherly" God who holds us morally responsible for all our sins and transgressions, with the only forgiveness through the Sacrament of Confession, with the power of a priest who may have recently come from sexually molesting an altar boy.

When I speak of the liberal or democratic vs the conservative republican persuasion, I am referring to the social/ emotional disposition, not the economic. The democratic lifestyle moves one toward the socialization of culture; that is, a sense of fairness and consideration for one's neighbors and working associates, just as we attempt to teach our children socialization skills and attitudes of cooperation. They value opportunity for all so that no one is deprived of a chance to succeed, as was the admonition of Adam Smith in his great book, *The Wealth of Nations*, in which he espoused the values of "moral sentiments and fellow feeling" when it came to the way in which people should conduct themselves in the interests of civility. They value opportunity for all and some thoughtful restraint over the amassing of extraordinary wealth and tax benefits that only favor the super-rich.

The conservative position seems to value a tightly held authoritarian system of stability, predictability, and a pre-established way of life that ensures law and order and established precedence, along with a psychological sense of self-sufficiency. It also favors minimal controls or regulations on business and industry while minimizing the power of strong labor unions—in other words, a "free and unfettered market" bereft of regulation, as promoted by figures such as Ayn Rand and Ronald Reagan.

At the same time, the conservative view fears that Liberalism promotes a creeping socialism in which all the nation's wealth would eventually be distributed equally among citizens, whether they earn it or not, and the government would control everything. This would never be tolerated in this country because it would stifle entrepreneurship and the incentive to produce and create, which are the driving forces of this economy.

There is such a fear of creeping socialism that even the most fundamental services of government — public education, medical coverage, national security, and interstate commerce —would be adversely affected and entirely subject to governmental authority. However, partial socialism is effectively functional in this country, as Social Security, Medicare, and Medicaid, and most people agree that this is a healthy component of our economic system because it provides some security for older people and those less fortunate than the rest of us. This system needs to be extended to universal medical coverage and education through college and even graduate school for deserving individuals, to enhance and safeguard the security and integrity of this country.

It may seem I have gone off the subject on this discourse. However, I am still talking about social/ emotional differences between attitude variances with regard to liberal and conservative, which, in my way of thinking, emanates from fundamental attitudes of seeing the world as secure or threatening and from a basic disposition of faith or belief systems. Can we be trusting or non-trusting?

Ancient societies were decidedly autocratic by necessity, and people deferred their inherent personal sovereignty to a monarch, king, sultan, pharaoh, pope, chief, guru, or other potentate deemed to have special powers of governance. Since people formed tribes for protection, someone had to be designated as a leader, and that person would have complete control to maintain the tribe's solidarity and unity. Punishment, pain, and exile were the means of enforcing the leader's rules. History is replete with examples of such societies that developed into distinct cultures and forms of communication.

The need for security (both physical and emotional) lies at the heart of our personhood. It must be addressed when we are in our formative years if we are to develop into well-socialized and socially responsible adults who function out of a faith in ourselves and in life rather than out of basic fear and insecurity. The degree of successful coping depends on the bedrock foundation of security we experience in our early developmental years. Suppose one experiences too much a lack of such security in childhood. In that case, he will likely clamor for some form of authority figure to guide and direct him, and to take responsibility for charting a course for his life, much as an autocratic leader would.

Some people prefer to live that way, but many do not. The abuse of the autocratic power will quite often lead to some form of rebellion or aggression toward others or oneself Juvenile Probation Officers, as I was at one time who work in the step-parent adoptions department, will tell you the tragic phenomenon of small children desperately trying to hang on to an abusive parent even though a loving step-parent is ready and willing to provide a providential borne to the abused child. Ideally, the best is to offer responsible leadership with accountability, as we try to do in democratic systems of government.

Two ways of looking at human personality development can be described analogously as "roots and wings" and are sometimes questionably established in our character development. Indigenous security is a condition so deeply rooted, emotionally, in our character as we grow from childhood to adulthood. Some of us are given firm "roots" as a foundation, but not the "wings" of independent development, and must rely later on some external form of authority to guide our emotional and spiritual lives, or no guidance whatsoever.

Opting for a continuation of this relationship is what produces the traditional conservative personality. As I see it, it is a perpetuation of what has already been established as laudable and reliable, even though by a dictatorial and or sometimes harsh pedagogical parent administration. However, there is another vital aspect of human life that must move forward into the unknown and the undiscovered, bringing us the benefits of modern medicine, communication, transportation, and technology, and a growing awareness of the possibilities of life on this planet and, indeed, in space itself.

However, it seems that during times of stress such as we are experiencing now with the upcoming general election for President and one of the candidates now being adjudicated in a New York Federal Court for one of several federal crimes, we tend to become more entrenched in the primary persuasions of how we choose to live and what we value because people can, unfortunately, digress into confusion and belligerency as it has with our federal administration and the Republican dominated US Congress. Either autocratic or democratic can go to extremes and amount to a combative disposition leading nowhere, and we wind up with hostile stagnation instead of intelligent cooperation looking for consensual agreement for the betterment of all.

We must learn to become more objective and circumspect at times like this so that emotionalism does not obscure, as Lincoln said, "the lights of our better angels."

So, how did we human beings get from where we were to where we are today? It seems humans, in general, have a disposition on the one hand to advance and generously support the society they live in for the betterment of all, and, on the other hand, some only wish to exploit what already exists for their own personal benefit and self-interest. People have written books on the self-interest, narcissistic pall that has descended on the US in the past several years since WWII, and this unwholesome digression has led one of our current candidates for President to express concern about "saving the soul of America." We seem to have devolved into a bifurcated society of those who would seek out what is only in their personal interests and those who want to sustain the Constitutional values on which this country was founded. The US has become a land of the exploiters and the exploited.

We, as a people, must recognize, as our forefathers did, that a democracy can only be sustained as a viable way of life if the rights, freedoms, and liberties we enjoy under such a government are sustained alongside the recognition of the responsibilities that sustain those rights and freedoms. Rights and freedoms without a recognition of the responsibilities that underlie those rights and freedoms are nothing but fantasy and destructive fantasy at that. This is the precarious position our country is in today.

The psychiatrist/ philosopher, Viktor Frankl, in his book, *Man's Search for Meaning* said, "without responsibleness" as he put it, "we are only expressing our felt civil rights," without recognizing that socialization is functional when we acknowledge that we can only accomplish and produce with the cooperation of others, i. e., management cannot produce without labor and labor cannot produce without management.

We cannot practice these ideals without recognizing that it takes an awareness and consideration of the needs and interests of others as well as ourselves." American society, today, has been called nihilistic and narcissistic, and hence almost to the point of self-destruction, so much so that we, as a people, cannot even trust our leaders in government to do what is right for our nation. There is so much self-interest under the guise of patriotic fervor that children no longer know with certainty just what this country stands for, and the cherished ideals that many Americans have sacrificed their lives for have become tarnished and even discarded.

I have no data or experimental design to back up what I am about to say regarding the authoritarian personality, but I do think there are clues about how we develop toward authoritarian dependency or toward a bold thrust toward progressive thinking and the individuation of character.

It has to do with the kind of pedagogical training one gets as a child. If the child is allowed a sense of freedom to express what he feels without threat and with a sense that what the child perceives about himself and what interests him and is respectfully regarded during the early stage of brain development, that emerging person will grow to have a strong sense of what he or she likes or values. Self-confidence grows from that kind of experience, and with that comes ease and confidence in becoming trustworthy and responsible. On the other hand, if the child is harshly prohibited from honoring and accepting his feelings and interests, he will feel threatened, and unable to develop a confident sense of him or herself, and will from then on be unable to function without a dependent personal character.

There are antecedents to child development that contribute to the development of an authoritarian personality. Samuel J. Warner, Ph.D. enumerated several of them. In his book, *Self-Realization and Self-Defeat,* he talks about frustrations in childhood that lead to some form of insecurity, which leads to some form of aggression and or super competitiveness, which, socially, is expressed as dominance/submission or control/ subservience or helplessness and hopelessness and despair or a possible life on the streets.

Suppose the frustration takes the form of aggressive hostility. In that case, a resentment will often build to the point of explosive violence as we frequently now see in the form of horrifying assaults on innocent people and even children in school with high-powered semi-automatic rifles with large capacity magazines that were designed for military combat, and/or the unfortunate individual will commit suicide.

Harry Stack Sullivan, the famous psychiatrist and psychoanalyst whose primary contribution to the field of child development was the idea of the "significant other" and how that significant person can impact the development of the child, mentions that an aggressive, competitive parent can set up an anxious/attachment relationship that causes a child to "maintain a feeling of safety only in the esteem reflected by the parent or another person because he does not have the inner emotional resources to provide his own self-esteem and therefore seeks it from another person" and this is often the basis of failed or sustaining narcissistic relationships.

Sullivan further talks about how narcissistic parenting will desire to be sufficiently effective: "So as to permit a proud display to the world as an extension of her own ego, yet there is a conflicting desire that the parent alone be intelligent and capable in the household. The result of this conflict is often a merciless goading of the child toward unattainable heights of accomplishment, an outward rejection of the child for not meeting these impossible standards, and inner resentment over the child's actual accomplishments and level of maturation. Such a child becomes neurotically anxious over signs of emerging capabilities and uniqueness. Impelled by his anxieties and wish for acceptance toward the never-never land of perfection and, hence, repelled from the dangerous possibilities of actual though mundane accomplishments, he settles for the safe haven of servitude and obeisance to authority and power. The authoritarian conscience, too, patterned after this parent, may be most protective and supportive when the adult invites the world, through his actions, to pity and despise him."

The solution to this dilemma is often dependence and submissiveness. According to Warner, "By giving up his will, by self-infantilization, he finds escape at least from parental rejection because of the competition implicit in maturation; although he is bound, in any event, to be disparaged and scorned for ineffectuality, fancied or real. Though yielding his initiative and integrity, submerging his volition and mental processes within another person, and assuming a passive-receptive relation to a larger and apparently stronger individual, he can participate in the will of the larger person, and sense a primitive omnipotence through annihilation of selfhood." This, I think, is the essence of the "authoritarian personality."

Warner goes on to further describe the kind of child development that we later see in the type of adult that becomes stunted in its reach for full functioning, independence, and individuation. He says: "We often find the parent who alternates between over-severity and spoiling, between unrealistic verbal super-evaluation and disparaging and shaming—the cause generally being a lack of genuine affection in the parent (who, for her or his own reason, is unable to give it). In its stead are found the inner alteration of hostility and guilt.

This sequence explains the outer alteration between lionizing the child as a rediscovered favorite toy and humiliating him as a necessary but much resented evil. The child's resulting self-concept and self-esteem are accordingly chaotic, and the infantilizing reluctance to yield to primitive power operations is therefore understandable in terms of defensive needs. Guilt and anxiety, on the part of the parent as a result of unfulfilled personal aspirations, can be projected on to a child in very destructive ways and results in a parent/child dynamic in which the parent chastises the child for not living up to an ideal of accomplishment and then, alternately, berates the child when it fails to live up to the parent's needs and expectations.

In such a case, the child feels never so safe with the competitive parent as when he or she is 'cute' and ineffectual, and never so in danger of rejection as when he or she manifests maturity and power. The authoritarian conscience, too, patterned after this parent, may be most protective and supportive when the adult invites the world, through his actions, to pity and despise him. Furthermore, where there is guilt, there will be a need to suffer. And where there is a need to suffer, innate intelligence will be perverted from creative goals and deflected toward a habitual fabrication of pits and snares for self-entrapment and self-hurt." To become truly comfortable with oneself, a child must feel uninhibitedly comfortable with his family.

Finally, Warner says, "If we select two groups of children, those with loving parents and those with essentially rejecting and competitive ones, we have analogues of the subjects. For the loved (and therefore emotionally secure) children will go through their developmental years under the pressures of hunger, self-realization, desire for companionship, sex, and so on; the unloved children will have, in addition to these pressures, the added anxiety of anticipating severe rejection concerning things which are beyond their control. Further, the highly anxious individual is less able to tolerate abstract or ambiguous situations.

He wants to know and to know definitely, for he is perplexed by too many unanswered questions emanating from the world within. He desires concreteness in the world without having to compensate for the inner indefiniteness, and to overbalance the ill-structured feelings which beset him—feelings which are severely disquieting and yet have no identifiable cause. This seems to be the underlying characteristic of the authoritarian personality that must have indisputable leadership and therefore is vulnerable to the persuasive arts of the consummate "con man."

PART II

Power
Infallibility
Obedience
LOVE & COMPASSION
Fear & Control
RENEW THE CHURCH
Faith, Dignity & Freedom

THE MISSION
PART II

Part I of my essay on Catholicism dealt with the abuses of power and control within the Church's institutional hierarchy. My position is that the Church had become more of a temporal/political entity than a spiritual/inspirational movement founded by Jesus Christ after the Donation of Constantine in the fourth century. During this time, there was a dispute over the authority of the Roman Church. Before he died, Constantine (as Emperor of the Holy Roman Empire) granted the Bishop of Rome, as inheritor of St. Peter, lands in Judea, Greece, Asia, Thrace, Africa, and the entire Western Roman provinces, while leaving Constantine with imperial authority in the Eastern Byzantine provinces with the intention of consolidating his Eastern Roman Empire.

So, what were the essentials of this great movement that inspired people to devote their lives and energy to this great cause? The second part of this essay is about the essential treasures of Christ's life and teachings and religion in general. What is the difference?

The difference is between a spiritual awakening and celebration of an inspirational and meaningful life on the one hand and, on the other, an institutional/religious persuasion of guilt, fear, and dogmatic dominance. The former reveres Christ for his life, teachings, and divine inspiration, while the latter glorifies Him for his death on the cross as an atonement for ancestral disobedience and for an afterlife of eternal union with God if one obeys the teachings of the institutional Church, or eternal damnation if one does not.

Catholicism and its teachings, as I came to know them as a young child growing up in the Catholic Church, is what I refer to as Catholic-ism. It has become, over the centuries, a rigid, authoritarian, and systematized bureaucracy that stifles rather than inspires a deep spirituality and union with the wonders of God through the personage of Christ (and others, I might add) as to the awesomeness of the universe we live in, and, indeed, life itself. Is it any wonder that some of the great Roman Catholic thinkers and artists of the early years of Papal Christianity were in contention with the Papal authority of the Roman Catholic Church?

Are we, as humans, alone in this mighty universe, or are we not? It is a mind-boggling thought to contemplate. Was our need to feel special and favored by God through the administration of the Church the reason that the Church's position held or dogmatized that our earth was the center of the Universe and all of it revolved around us, like the infant's perception of himself or herself as being the center of everything?

Some might question the value of religion. Why is religion important to the human species in the first place? Has it not led to many brutal wars and oppressive impositions? These are very valid questions, it seems to me.

Once again, let me reiterate my understanding of the difference between Catholic-ism and what I call Catholicity. To my way of thinking, it is this:

Catholicism represents the traditions, dogmas, and formal protocols of the institution we have come to know as the Catholic Church, both the Eastern and Western branches. This, as I referenced before, goes back to the early days of the Roman Church under the rule of Constantine. It is the politico/religious structure of what constituted the expansion of the authority of the Bishop of Rome into a sovereign state with all its political tributaries.

Catholicity, on the other hand, conceives of the mission of Christ as the unifying movement of all of God's creatures into a recognition of the dignity, value, and spiritual dimension of life and of all things. Instead of partitioning people into sects based on religious belief systems. It includes all people into one unified spiritual organism and unifies and includes all (as in the word catholic) rather than separates and distinguishes. To think of all humanity as an organism is to acknowledge this phenomenon from the inception of the primordial cells of life by genetic disposition and the process of mitosis, in which cells begin a selective division into what will become the cells that make up the eyes, heart, lungs, and so forth.

The eventual result will become a fully functional organism we call a human being. This same fully developed human being will further select a function to contribute to the overall functioning of the society in which he or she lives. So, we have mechanics, artists, physicians, bankers, farmers, and so forth. We do not have everyone wanting to do the same thing. Each contributes to the overall value and purpose of life. This is why I call humanity an "organism." We have a conglomerate that, together, maintains and enhances the entire phenomenon of life.

This, however, is not to deny the various cultural persuasions that deal with secular life. The substance of religion, however, deals with the spiritual values that Christ and others talked about when He mentioned "the bread of Life."

Religion is not a mysterious thing. It is indigenous to mankind as "a binding back to the God of its creation." As far back as recorded history and beyond that, as Cultural Anthropology tells us, and from remnants of archaeological studies of ancient settlements, we find that humans built altars and made engravings of beings somewhat like themselves but somehow different. It can be inferred that these images and altars had a special purpose, and it is believed that they were used to pay homage to great powers or gods who held grave influences over their livelihoods and destinies.

Primitive men and women must have feared events in their lives that could be destructive or protective but were beyond their control and management, so it was not unreasonable to believe that there were great powers controlling events they could not control. It seemed natural for these individuals to project beings capable of managing and controlling natural catastrophes and, like themselves, appeasable if given proper respect and deference. These powerful beings could be offered gifts and homage in this regard, just as an elder with power over them could be appeased with gifts and honors.

When these people evolved to the point of learning to grow crops of food and also manage animals for their sustenance, they must have beseeched their "Gods" to favor them with good harvests and healthy animals along with their own well-being. It seems that in the minds of these people, there could be good gods and bad gods because some happenings were beneficent and some were destructive and devastating, and members of their own tribe experienced these inclinations in their own lives as well as in other tribes who sought to destroy them or overpower them.

Later, in the dawn of written history, some wise men conceived of documenting their sense of the god/man relationship, and thus emerged the ancient conception of Genesis and how this relationship developed. Notions of good and evil began to appear in this dominant/submissive relationship.

These early writers conceived of a divine garden in which early man (Adam and his mate Eve) enjoyed a close "fatherly" relationship with the divine protector and benefactor, with one stipulation: that they demonstrate their obedience to their God by not eating of the "fruit of the tree of knowledge of good and evil" as in some interpretations. Since these two disobeyed their God and fell out of his grace, they were to know the dark side of life by becoming estranged from their Godly father. This, it seems to me, is the beginning of the frightful existence that humans must navigate through the world alone with the realization that they have lost their relationship with God, the divine benefactor and protector.

Here, now, is the realization that religion (or a binding back to god—Latin derivative) was to become a universal mandate for all generations to come in one form or another. Along with the imperative need to reconnect with God was the dire need to disassociate oneself from those who seemed not to have the will or sanction for this divine connection. Those who seemed not to have this divine connection were perceived as evil, threatening, and aligned with evil forces.

There were epic struggles between good and evil and dire efforts to regain the good graces of god.

The enormity of the human preoccupation to regain a relationship with the protective father developed all over the world as humans became more aware of their vulnerable existence. Some cultures found venerable personages, such as Buddha in China, Vishnu in India, Mohammed in Arabia, and Christ in Jerusalem. From these came offshoots and hybrid tributaries.

Even in the isolated South Sea Islands, the natives erected stamens and various artifacts of worship. It is interesting to note that the isolated primitive tribes, whether in the Pacific or in Africa, did not seem to get the notion of evil or evil gods, but instead sought to appease the gods like children beseeching their father for favors and protection, even though some were very aggressive and warlike.

Always contingent on this sought-after relationship with God was the intrusion of the awful awareness of good and evil in the world, which was ever present, whether in natural catastrophic events or the terrible manifestations of human brutality. The Hebrew religion took the form of numerous, stringent laws to avoid evil. Sacrifices became a common way of showing deference to god—even by slaying the best and 'most innocent of their tribe. Even Abraham, the most revered patriarch of the

Jewish people, was obediently prepared to slay his son at the behest of God until restrained at the last minute by an interposing angel.

An exciting development in the evolution of human awareness was the contribution of the early Greeks. Aristotle, who was a student of Plato, who, in turn, was a student of Socrates, developed concepts of a "soul" —a part of life that transcended the material. Aristotle described this concept as "prime matter and substantial form." Plato also took this notion and described human life as a reflection of the true state of being, which was incorporeal, and Socrates believed the soul is immortal. He also argued that death is not the end of existence; it is merely a separation of the soul from the body.

When Jesus of Nazareth came on the scene, the notion of binding more intimately with God took on more intensity as it rubbed up against the "pagan" notions of projected gods as the Romans had conjured up. During this period in history it is interesting to note that according to Professor Bart D. Ehsman, University of North Carolina at Chapel Hill, in the Great Courses book, *How Jesus Became God*, he states that "the ancient world knew of more than one mortal who was thought to be the Son of God, such as the pagan philosopher Appollonius of Tyana who came along 50 years after Christ and was thought to have had very similar characteristics, such as virgin birth, healing the sick and raising the dead. The point being that at that time in history, there seemed to be a frenzy of attributing superhuman powers to ordinary people or those thought to be extraordinary.

As Christianity began to emerge from the fertile soil of Judaism and gathered a devout following, significant controversies developed as to whether Christ was God or whether he was an ordinary human being who became God, or whether he was God who became a man with Divine powers. The Jews rejected the whole idea of Jesus being the Messiah because they had expected the Messiah to come to lead them. Apparently, in their view, the Messiah was to be a great and powerful leader who would exalt His "chosen people" over the pagan Roman supremacy of Caesar, who, himself, was thought to be a god.

The whole issue was not settled until the Council of Nicaea in 325 AD under the auspices of Constantine, who sought further unification of his Empire through a consensus of the Churchmen. Arianism was a big issue about the nature of Christ and that had to be resolved. It was resolved in favor of Christ being identified with God, but it left dissension among the ranks of the Church. Later, at the Council of Chalcedon in 451 AD, the issue was somewhat settled when it was agreed that Christ was both man and God. Those in the East, however, were not completely satisfied with the amount of power and authority the Roman Church claimed, and there was much contention between East and West until, "on Saturday, July 16, 1054, as afternoon prayers were about to begin, Cardinal Humbert, legate of Pope Leo IX, strode into the Cathedral of Hagia Sophia, right up to the main alter, and placed on it a parchment that declared the Patriarch of Constantinople, Michael Cerularious, to be excommunicated. He then marched out of the Church, shook the dust from his feet, and left the city: A week later, the patriarch solemnly condemned the cardinal" (1054 The East-West Schism-George T. Denais of Christian History)

It is thought, however, by most that the underlying reasons for the split were because the Western church called for the strengthening of papal authority, which caused the church to become more autocratic and centralized. Basing his claims on his succession from St. Peter, the pope asserted his direct jurisdiction over the entire church, East as well as West.

In the Middle East around the early 600s, according to *The Historical Atlas of the Mediterranean: The Rise of Islam*, a young man named Muhammad began declaring that he was receiving messages from God and that he was a prophet in the same line as Jesus and Moses. At first, the Pagan Arabs were tolerant and even curious about the new "prophet." They had a genuine interest in the monotheistic beliefs of the Jews and Christians and were willing to make room for another religious belief system in their society. It was not until Muhammad began insulting the traditional Pagan deities and insisting that the Pagan Arabs and their ancestors would burn in hell for eternity for worshipping false gods that they began to regard Muhammad and his followers with disdain.

He and his followers were eventually forced to move from Mecca to Medina in 622 where he set up operations to raid the merchant caravans along their route. He gathered followers by promising them eternal paradise in the afterlife if they joined him in his battles against both the Pagan, Jewish, and Arab tribes.

Over time, divisions developed among the Islamic people, i.e., the Shia and the Sunni sects. In terms of leadership, the Shia held that leadership must come by inheritance directly from Mohammed, while the Sunni, which represents about 85% of the Islamic population, took the position that leadership must be earned by proving oneself worthy and capable. These bifurcations are not uncommon. When you look at traditional Roman and Byzantine Catholic and then Roman Catholic and Protestant, Jewish Orthodox and Jewish Reform, even political divisions of reactionary conservative and radical liberal, there is a pronounced tendency on the part of human nature to want to stay close to the familiar and traditional, on the one hand, and the desire to move forward on the other. There have been militant elements in Judeo/Christianity, as in the Crusades and the Inquisition, during the early establishment of the new religion, which was sanctioned by Papal decree to fortify and defend itself against those who would oppose it.

In Islam, as it was in Christianity, Martyrdom was considered a divinely inspired way to please God by remaining true to the faith. Whether this is delusional thinking or not can be debated, but that is the way it was. I am not persuaded that Islamic leadership is dedicated to the destruction of Western Civilization, although there are elements that do, just as early Christianity sought to Christianize the world. Perhaps, Islam, being a younger religion, is also going through stages of evolution that Christianity had gone through much earlier.

Raza Aslam, in his book, *No god but God*, points out how different sects have interpretations that are demeaning and punitive, while others are more considerate and respectful. In another book by Irshad Manji titled *The Trouble with Islam Today*, she is urging those of her religion to reform the faith, empower women, encourage independent thinking, and respect the views of others.

Following the evolution of Christianity as the bulwark in the development of Western Civilization, we find a modernization in the codification of laws of faith emerging through the Protestant movement started by Martin Luther against the intractable dogmas of Catholic-ism. On the one hand, one may not be required to commune with God through the priest, while on the other, it is maintained as an absolute necessity through the Catholic Sacraments, one can pray to God but not receive his sanctified benefits unless in conformity with the Catholic mandated Sacraments of Christ.

So, despite its rigid structure, what can we learn from the historical development of the Catholic Church and all religions? We can trace the concept of the "high feed-low road" dichotomy from the ancient Greeks, whose philosophy conceived of the Apollonian god (rational thinking, order, and appealing to prudence and purity) and the Dionysian god (irrationality, chaos, emotions, and instinct), both of whom were the sons of Zeus.

In the Far East, philosophical/religious sentiments were expressed through the concepts of Yin and Yang (the dark and bright sides of man). In modern times, Psychology has empirically and scientifically identified the brain functions of the right hemisphere and forebrain, which more or less govern whether we are functioning in a cerebral (cognitive) or emotional (affective) way. One stresses reason and the other, feeling and emotion. Reason can guide us while emotion can lead us astray; however, it is mainly through emotion that we enjoy the richness and pleasures of life.

In Freudian terms, it is the constant tug-of-war between the id (seeking only one's own pleasures and satisfaction) and the superego (adhering only to the admonitions of parental and imposed authority), with the ego being the mediator between the two. The ego is the function that maintains a stable attitude, rewards reality, and helps one acquire one's needs, personal interests, and desires in a balanced and socialized way.

It seems to me that these concepts and understandings of human nature are the stuff of religion—that is, we must recognize the aspirations of goodness as well as the frailty that is underlying the basic needs for physiological and emotional security, belongingness, love, and productivity—a fulfilled and gratifying life with a hope for some extension of existence beyond this life.

Shakespeare said, "What dreams may come when we have shuffled off this mortal coil." The human being is a marvelous creature of God, and He must be in total affirmation of His creations since God cannot create something and then reject it or create a human being that He knew beforehand was destined to go to hell and eternal domination. That would be rejecting Himself.

I speak in personification terms, but I really don't understand the mystery of all of these things; however, I do believe in something quite beyond our understanding that accounts for all things, and it is reflected in human goodness, wisdom, altruism, and compassion for ourselves as well as others. In a human sense and in the universe in an existential sense, I agree with St. Thomas Aquinas, who said that evil is the absence of good, and for this we must seek to understand in both a cognitive and an active way why such absence of good exists in Man. This is the domain of psychology and religion since they both deal with the spirit and soul of Man. I don't think it can be attributed to a devil or satanic influences as though humans fall into evil ways due to some outside spiritual personage driving them in a direction alien to their essential being, which, having been created by God, cannot be anything but good.

To deny that God is the creator of good is to affirm that He is the creator of evil, and that belies everything that speaks of what is true. God, as conceived of as the Supreme Authority of all things who is thought to be all good, all omniscient, and all powerful, cannot conceivably create a human being so corrupted and disinclined toward its own good that such a person is doomed to spend eternity in everlasting hell and damnation. That defies rational thinking, and, after all, we are made with the potential for intelligence and mindfulness.

I speak as though God is a person; however, I don't conceive of God as such, but rather the ultimate creator of all the universe and of all things, whatever that is. In my mind, I associate God with goodness that I see in well-developed human beings and that I see as a reflection of our creator.

The Church's mission, it seems to me, is to foster and support the high road of spirituality and goodness through the inspiration of the Holy Spirit, but with the acknowledgement of our human frailty, i.e, our imperfections and experiential bondage to "poisonous pedagogy" of faulty parenting and tutelage.

We must not be diminished or condemned for the Dionysian part of our nature as well as the Apollonian, but encouraged to learn and grow into a fuller humanness and appreciation of our existence. Part of maturing spiritually, as well as organically and intellectually, is not to be diminished by our low road motivations but ennobled by them as we learn to synergize all dimensions of ourselves into a unity of glorification of our existence.

Some of the outstanding achievements in the annals of human history stem from the influence of the great religions. These spiritual endeavors were prompted, I believe, by the synergistic integration of intellect and passion, of religious maturity and growth, and of struggles to raise humanity above the "slings and arrows of outrageous fortune," and to seek a more hopeful destiny. Religious maturity and growth, it seems to me, is stifled and stultified by unyielding influences of rigid dogma and untampered tradition. We must be unbound so that we can truly have the courage to love with the fullness of our being. Consider such great artists as Leonardo da Vinci, Michelangelo, and Rafael, who struggled with the Papal decree.

Scientists such as Galileo and Pasteur and the great father of the Church, St. Augustine, who struggled with baser passions that had to become tempered with his great intelligence to achieve a synergy of excmplary religious contribution, Some of the great religious music such as the Bach B minor mass, Gregorian Chants and Madrigals, Beethoven's Missa Solemnis, the Mass in C Major, and the Berlioz Requiem and the Te Deum, all created and produced with great passion and reverence for the Divine.

The great cathedrals, such as the Piazza del Duomo and its magnificent dome, created and engineered by Filippo Brunelleschi of Florence, and other great cathedrals in Europe, inspired works in passionate praise of the God of their understanding. It seems to me that the positive side of religion inspires toward peace, love, and hope for better things to come. In contrast, the negative side creates fear, guilt, and shame, and a defensive withdrawal from life into a delusional cocoon of exclusivity and rigid dogmas, and that often leads to violent confrontations or internal pathological behavior such as the abuse of children and heretical persecutions, crime, and war.

Is it possible to satisfy the spiritual dimension of our lives while we are in the process of living, that does not offend or insult our God given intelligence with delusional belief systems and anxieties about our final disposition? Happy children don't fret about such things if they feel secure and cared for. They open themselves up to the wonders of life and living. I think somewhere in the Bible, Christ was said to proclaim, "Be as little children." I think he must have meant not to be childish in our behavior but to be open to living in our spirits.

Perhaps the key to living fully and without feelings of guilt, fear and shame s to experience our early lives with the love and caring that emanated from the spirit of Christ as a model for "parenting" ourselves and as well as our children in a way that allows for continual development to our full potential as human—rather than a stultifying existence doggedly trying to stay aligned and obedient to a rigid authority of pre-fabricated rules and mandates. If it is true that God, whatever God is, created all of us and everything, and I am persuaded that it's so, then God will see to our final destiny, whatever it may be. Why vex over it?

This brings me to how we "parent" ourselves to live our lives fully with love, intelligence, and compassion for ourselves and others. It seems to me that we are living at a time when the human species has evolved to a point where knowledge and skill are moving us in the direction where all people on earth can live lives of satisfaction and productivity if we have enough sense to elect and follow leaders with wisdom and compassion and use our resources for the good of all. This is not only consistent with the best of religious sentiment but also in line with sound psychological sense.

First of all, I think we should put more effort into trying to understand the whys and wherefores of the nature of evil thinking and behavior rather than wasting energy with a preoccupation about the "devil" or "satanic forces" being at the root of all our troubles on earth.

That really will get us nowhere but more worry, anxiety, and distressful thinking. It will also lead us into hostile contentions with others because we will want to attribute what we don't like or understand about others as being deserving of destruction or, at least, avoidance and exclusion.

We are now at a point where we can begin to understand the true nature of why some of us move in the direction of anti-social attitudes and evil behavior, and how we can curtail and divert these tendencies in children as they go through their developmental stages of maturation. It all depends on good and effective parenting that allows for an appreciation of the innate child and bis/her own spiritual, emotional, and physical being. We must truly guide and model for our children what is true and good, rather than force and superimpose a matrix of attitudes and beliefs that our ancestors believed was right. Those who came before lived in a different era, so we must be open to the evolution and greater awareness of the human species. The worldview of those who lived in the time of Moses is not appropriate for those who live today. The world is not thought to be flat anymore, and our planet is not the center of the universe.

I envision religion as a spiritual and ethical component of our daily life in which there is no dogma or belief systems but, rather an active faith and hope in whatever condition of life we are in at the moment, we can be sure that wherever we are in life at the moment, we are meant to be there as a way station on our way to our ultimate destiny. God is ever in the world, and Jesus was a self-designated emissary because we chose it that way. I think Christ was trying to show us the way of light in our struggle for spiritual fulfillment as are so many others if we attend to such things.

If we teach our children that life, with all its struggles and disappointments, is still a purposeful endeavor, and everyone is a contributor as in an organism that has function and purpose, then those who aspire toward a religious vocation, rather than being ordained as in an inherited chain of sancti-fied authority, would be dedicated to inspiring and guiding people along their path of spiritual enlight-enment. Rather than compulsory attendance at Church under the coercion of the threat of damna-tion, one could think of assemblies of like-minded people who reinforce their devotion to living the good life and manifesting high moral and ethical standards for their children.

Someone once said that in India, where she was raised in a Christian school, the lessons were on the "science of ethics and morality" rather than routine readings from the Gospel because those con-siderations cut across all religious persuasions. It seems to me that those were excellent lessons to learn within the realm of spiritual awareness. In the minds of many of the Judeo-Christian faith, the Bible is the absolute keystone of everything religious.

Many believe it is the absolute literal Words of God. Some of us, as I do, believe the Bible is the record of our ancient ancestors as to their perceived relationship with what they conceived of as their God—the Creator. Thus, we have ancestral stories, Psalms, accumulated wisdom, admonitions of right and wrong, concepts of punishment and justice, divine interventions, and historical events.

In the New Testament, a new concept of the same God in the personhood of Christ was to enlighten people as to a new awareness of a more purposeful life and a God of forgiveness and compassion. Even though Christ taught about God, he seemed to think of himself more as a son of God rather than the Son of God. Some people say he was God because he worked miracles, but so did Elijah of the Hebrew Bible and Jesus's Jewish contemporary, Hanina Hen Dosa, as well as Oral Roberts in modern times. In my view, all these testimonials of the ancients were the perceptions of people whose knowledge, experiences, and perceptions were shaped by their times and reflect those times. Their written thoughts and beliefs were their gift to the progeny that came after, I believe, and were meant to advise and provide meaning and wisdom, but not a way of life cast in stone.

Why did the early Church fathers, under the leadership of Constantine I, decide to choose only the gospels of Matthew, Mark, Luke, and John when John's gospel is in disagreement with the others? Why were all the other gospels discarded or held as unreliable? Why was Peter's gospel not given the same credibility as the first four mentioned above, and yet Peter was chosen to represent Christ on earth in the personhood of Papal (Vicar of Christ) authority?

In my opinion, the wisdom, teachings, and spiritual purpose of Christ preceded the gospels. After all, the one written closest to Christ's death was written by John, approximately 60 years after the death of Christ, and those who study such things are not even sure that those who were alleged to have written the gospels were in fact the ones who wrote them. Perhaps the persuasive power of Jesus of Nazareth was the embodiment of a spiritual movement that would set humanity on an uplifting path of hope and compassion, and an awareness of human potential for expansion with an unbounded destiny. We can see that with the advent of Catholicity in conflict with Catholic-ism, as an adversary, humanity has grown and developed into a magnificent culture of scientific and religious progress despite the drag of stultifying dogmatic institutionalism.

So, what have I learned from all this, and what do I wish for my children? I have learned that I have spent most of my life as an excessively passive person, looking toward the Church, someone, or something outside of myself for purpose and direction. I bowed down in fear to authority and at the same time rebelled against it. I spent too much time waiting and looking to others, listening to others, and even blaming others because of my fear of taking responsibility for my own judgments, authenticity, and validation. I don't blame those who raised me, nor do I blame myself; however, I have felt responsible to do what I can to remedy the attitudes we lived with that, in my opinion, were unhealthy and developmentally arresting.

We can only do what we think is best at the time and what our awareness allows us to understand. In this regard, I have also learned that each child faces a critical dilemma. As the child begins to discover him or herself, they must decide how to respond to parental reflections. If the parent responds with intimidating threats against the child's own emerging selfhood, then that child will arrest its own development so as to secure its own safety, rather than honor itself. The child will consequently incorporate an underlying anxiety of self-doubt, and as will consequently follow, the person in authority will be fearful of realizing their own potential and, with age, will look back with depression or regret at a life of unfulfilled promise. If the child is on a quest for continued self-awareness and growth, it will feel encouraged to do so and will therefore grow into a fully functioning human being.

As Abraham Maslow put it in his book, *Toward A Psychology of Being*, published in 2014, "The primal choice, the fork in the road, then, is between others' and one's own self. If the only way to maintain the self is to lose to others, then the ordinary child will give up the self; this is true for the reason already mentioned: safety is a most basic and potent need for children, more necessary by far than independence and self-actualization. If adults force this choice upon him, of choosing between the loss of one (lower) vital necessity or another (higher) vital necessity, the child must choose safety even at the cost of giving up self and growth. "

Arrested childhood development is not a hopeless situation, but it does entail a life of struggle and extraordinary effort to break through the defeatist mentality. It also requires the support of others along the way.

With respect to my children, it would be my hope and wish that they would take from what I have written about my life toward an understanding that they have a fundamental right to their own judgments, authenticity, and validation, but not with an attitude of arrogance. I have learned that I need a faith, but a faith that does not betray my intelligence and good sense—a faith in which I can accept the part of me that was raised as a Catholic and yet not allow myself to become victimized and intimidated by it through guile, fear, and shame.

There are parts I can take from what I have come to learn from that religion, but not the institutional hierarchy and dogma that come with it. I reject an identification with the term Catholicism but do identify with the term Christian Catholicity because the former suggests institutional rigidity and authoritarian oppression, while the latter suggests an exaltation of the human spirit in a trusting and growing relationship with God.

These are my views and opinions. I only claim the freedom to think my thoughts and express them as I see fit. I think the essence of what I write can be summed up in a few simple religious expressions, such as:

Paul's letter to the Corinthians while in Ephesus. – Corinthians 13

"If I speak in the tongues of men or of angels, but do not have love, I am only a resounding gong or a clanging cymbal. If I have the gift of prophecy and can fathom all mysteries and all knowledge, and if I have a faith that can move mountains, but do not have love, I am nothing. If I give all I possess to the poor and give over my body to hardship that I may boast, but do not have love, I gain nothing. Love is patient, love is kind. It does not envy, it does not boast, it is not proud. It does not dishonor others, it is not self-seeking, it is not easily angered, it keeps no record of wrongs. Love does not delight in evil but rejoices with the truth. It always protects, always trusts, always hopes, always perseveres. Love never fails. But where there are prophecies, they will cease; where there are tongues, they will be stilled; where there is knowledge, it will pass away.

For we know in part and we prophesy in part, but when completeness comes, what is in part disappears. When I was a child, I talked like a child, I thought like a child, I reasoned like a child. When I became a man, I put the ways of childhood behind me. For now we see only a reflection as in a mirror; then we shall see face to face. Now I know in part; then I shall know fully, even as I am fully known. And now these three remain: faith, hope and love. But the greatest of these is love."

THE PRAYER OF ST. FRANCIS OF ASSISI

Lord God, make me an instrument of thy peace. Where there is hatred, let me sow love. Where there is injury, pardon. Where there is doubt, faith. Where there is despair, hope. Where there is darkness, light. Where there is sadness, joy. Grant that I may not so much seek; to be consoled as to console, to be understood as to understand, to be loved as to love, for it is in giving that we receive and in pardoning that we are pardoned.

So how do I understand love and obedience?

Love, setting aside the hormonal imperatives and the fanciful and visceral affinities of youth, is courageous affirmation and caring kindness for one-self and others with appreciation of the wonders of

God's universe. Its effects are trusting relationships, faith in one's existence, hope in the future, and confidence and faith in one's own personhood.

Obedience can be taught as a fearful and coercive honoring and acquiescence to authority, or it can be taught with a desire to follow a trusted authority, such as when a child turns toward the sound of its mother or father's voice --- as though coming from a source of love and trust.

Finally, I would like to say that what I have written is not a condemnation of the Catholic Church (i.e. the body of the Church which is the people) but an honest attempt to deal with my own confusions and consternation as well as what seems feasible to hold with meaning and truth as I see it. Having grown up in the Church I have experienced many good people including priests and nuns as well as those not so good. There is the good and bad, the faulted and the un-faulted and that is just the reality of life. We develop institutions and hierarchies of authority to help us strive for better order and civility, however, it is also a reality that these institutions we create can also become rigid and destructive and therefore stifle our natural growth struggle for better light. It is my contention that this is what has happened to the Catholic Church as an institution and that is what must be ameliorated for it to manifest itself as a viable and thriving element in human life.

This book is about the evolution of the institutional Catholic Church which Pope Francis referred to as "a love story." Although it probably seems audacious of me to make such challenges of a Church that goes back in history for over 2000 years, I stand with the ranks of those raised as Catholic who have been dismayed, confused and deeply offended by the abusive activities of the hierarchy in willfully overlooking and deliberately minimizing the spiritual and moral trust of Catholic children.

READING MATERIAL

Armstrong, Karen (1993), *A History of God: The 4000-Year Quest of Judaism, Christianity and Islam.* New York, NY: Random House.

Asian, Reza (2005), *No god But God*; New York, Random House Trade Paperbacks, Avery, Peter and John Heath Stubbs; translated by (1979) *The Rubaiyat of Omar Khayyam*: New York, Penguin Books

Berry, Jason & Renner, Gerald (2004), *Vows of Silence; The Abuse of Power in the Papacy of John Paul II*, New York, Free Press

Bianchi, Eugene C. (2008), *The Children's Crusade; Scandal at the Vatican*; Thiensville, Wisconsin, Caritas Communications

Bradshaw, John (1988), *The Family; A Revolutionary Way of Self-Discovery;* Health Communications, Deerfield Beach, FIL

Brunsman, Father Barry (1986), *New Hope for Divorced Catholics:* Washington DC, Confraternity of Christian Doctrine

Bugliosi, Vincent (2011), *Divinity of Doubt;* New York, NY, Vanguard Press

Campbell, Joseph (1949), *The Hero with a Thousand Faces*; New York, Bollingen Foundation, Princeton University Press

Carroll, James (2002), *Toward a New Catholic Church;* New York, A Mariner Book, Houghton Mifflin Company

Carroll, James (2001), *Constantine's Sword; The Church and the Jews*, New York, A Mariner Book, Houghton Mifflin Company

Castaneda, Carlos (1998), *The Active Side of Infinity:* New York, Harper Collins Publishing.

Cronin, AJ. (1941), *The Keys of the Kingdom;* New York, Little Brown & Co.

Daniels, Susan, Ph.D., and Piechowski, Michael M., Ph.D. (2008), *Living With the intensity understanding the sensitivities, excitability, and*

Emotional Development of Gifted Children. Adolescents and Adults; Great Potential Press, Scottsdale, AZ

De Dijn, Herman (1996), *Spinaza: The Way to Wisdom*, Purdue University Press

Douglas, Kirk (1997), *Climbing the Mountain*; New York: A Touchstone Book

Erikson, Erik (1969), *Gandhi's Truth*; New York, WW. Norton & Company

Erikson, Erik and Robert Coles, M.D. (2001), *The Erik Erikson Reader;* New York, W. Norton & Company

Erikson, Erik (1950), *Childhood and Society*: New York, New York, WW. Norton & Company

Farquharson, A.S.L; translated by (1992), *Meditations of Marcus Aurelius*; New York, Alfred A. Knopf

Feiler, Bruce (2001), *Walking The Bible;* New York, Harper Collins Publishing

Follett, Ken (1989), *The Pillars of the Earth;* London, Penguin Books, Ltd.

Frankl, Viktor E. (2006), *Man's Search for Meaning:* Boston, Massachusetts, Beacon Press

Frawley-O'Dea, Mary Gail (2007), *Perversion of Power; Sexual Abuse in The Catholic Church*; Nashville, Vanderbilt University Press

Frost, S.E. (1942). *Basic Teachings of the Great Philosophers*; New York: Anchor Books Gibran, Kahlil (1997), The Prophet: New York, Alfred A. Kn

Goleman, Daniel (1995), *Emotional Intelligence*: New York, Random House

Goleman, Daniel (2006), *Social Intelligence*: 1 New York, Random House

Gottman, John Ph.D. (1995), *Why Marriages Succeed or Fail,* New York, Simon & Schuster

Gray, John (1999), *Children are From Heaven: Positive Parenting Skills for Raising Cooperative, Confident and Compassionate Children*, New York, Harper Collins Publisher

Hales, Dianne & Hales, Robert E., M.D. (1996), *Caring for the Mind; The Comprehensive Guide to Mental Health*; New York, Bantam Books

Hollis, James (1940), *Swamplands of the Soul*; Toronto, Canada, Inner City Books

Iscarior, Benjamin (2007), *The Gospel According to Judas*; New York, St. Martin's Press

James, William (2007), *The Varieties of Religious Experience:* Edinburgh, Scotland New Visions Publications

Kisch. Jonathan (2006), *A History of the End of the World: How the Most Controversial Book in the Bible Changed the Course of Western Civilization*; New York, Harper, San Francisco

B. Larson, M.D. (2001) *Handbook of Religion and Health*; New York, Oxford University Press

Lewis, C.S. (1943), *Mere Christianity*; New York, Collier Books

MacCallock, Diannaid (2009), *A History of Christianity*: London, England, Penguin Books

McCourt, Frank (1999), *Angela's Ashes*; New York, Touchstone

McGreal, Tan P. (Editor) (1992), *Great Thinkers of the Western World*: New York, Harper Resource

Miller, Alice (1980), *For Your Own Good: Hidden Cruelty in Child Rearing and The Roots of Violence*; Farrar, Straus and Giroux, New York, NY

Nolte, Dorothy Law (1998), *Children Learn What They Live*: New York, NY, Workman Publishing Company; Inc.

Redfield, James (1993), *The Celestine Prophecy*: New York, Warner Books

Siegel, Daniel J. M.D. and Hartzell, Mary, M.Ed. (2004), *Parenting from the Inside Qut: How a Deeper Understanding Can Help You Raise Children Who Thrive*, Penguin Random House, New York, NY

John Shelby, Bishop, (2009*), Eternal Life: A New Vision; Beyond Religion, Beyond Theism, Beyond Heaven and Hell;* New York, NY, Harper Collins

Shenon, Philip, (2005), *Jesus Wept;* Alfred A. Knopf, New York, NY, Random House

Stone, Irving (2004), *The Agony and the Ecstasy*: New York, The New American Library

Strauss, David Friedrich, Dr. (1912) (originally published in 1902) *The Life of Jesus Critically Examined*: London, Forgotten Books

Venden, Morris L. (1987), *Theses on Righteousness by Faith; Apologies to Martin Luther;* Nampa, Idaho, Pacific Press Publishing Association

Watts, Victor, translator; (1969), Boethius: *The Consolation of Philosophy;* London, Penguin Books

Waley, Arthur; translated by; (1938), *The Analects of Confucius;* New York, Vantage Books

Webb, James T. Ph.D. (2013), *Searching for Meaning: Idealism, Bright Minds, Disillusionment, and Hope*, Great Potential Press, Tucson, AZ

Winell, Malene Ph.D. (1993), *Leaving the Fold;* Berkeley, CA, Apocryphile Press

Waley, Arthur; translated by; (1938), *The Analects of Confucius;* New York, Vantage Books

Webb, James T. Ph.D. (2013), *Searching for Meaning: Idealism, Bright Minds, Disillusionment, and Hope,* Great Potential Press, Tucson, AZ

Winell, Malene Ph.D. (1993), *Leaving the Fold;* Berkeley, CA, Apocryphile Press